Activate 1

enquiries into local citizenship

Jim Hudson and
Suzanne Erlewyn-Lajeunesse
General editor: Lee Jerome

INSTITUTE FOR
CITIZENSHIP

Published in 2002 by:
Nelson Thornes Ltd
Delta Place
27 Bath Road
CHELTENHAM
GL53 7TH
United Kingdom

03 04 05 06 / 10 9 8 7 6 5 4 3 2

A catalogue record for this book is available from the British Library

ISBN 0-7487-6019-9

Illustrations by Peters & Zabransky, Bill Piggins and Liz Roberts
Designed by Clare Park

Printed and bound in China by Sun Fung

Acknowledgements

The Institute for Citizenship and Nelson Thornes have developed the Activate! range of resources to provide a comprehensive response to the national curriculum for Citizenship at Key Stage 3. Activate! includes the following components:

Teacher's Starter File
Textbooks
Photocopiable resource pack
CD-Rom
On-line case studies

All have been developed in close consultation with teachers and the case studies and Starter File are the results of an extensive two-year pilot project.

The Institute for Citizenship is an independent charitable trust that works to promote informed active citizenship and greater participation in democracy and society. It was established in 1992 by the then Speaker of the House, the Rt Hon Bernard Weatherill, MP. The Institute develops and pilots innovative citizenship education resources, undertakes research and seeks to stimulate debate around citizenship issues. The work of the Institute for Citizenship is made possible through a wide range of local and national partnerships.

For further information visit www.citizen.org.uk

The Institute for Citizenship would like to thank Bhavini Algarra for additional material and would like to acknowledge the support of the following organisations:

The Bridge House Estates Trust Fund
The Equitable Charitable Trust
J P Morgan Fleming Educational Trust
Hackney Local Education Authority
Halton Borough Council

The authors and publishers wish to thank the following for permission to reproduce photographs and other copyright material in this book:
p 12 (bottom right) Photofusion/Paul Baldesare; p 13 (bottom right) Rex Features/Erik Pendzich; p 16 Photofusion/Peter Olive; p 24 (left) Photofusion/Rob Scott, (right) Rex Features/Steve Lyne; p 48 (top left) Photofusion/Nicky Johnston, (bottom left) Photofusion/Lynne Connelly; p 57 Still Pictures/Ron Giling.

Every effort has been made to contact copyright holders. The publishers apologise to anyone whose rights have been inadvertently overlooked, and will be happy to rectify any errors or omissions.

Contents

Finding out

Where can you get information?

To understand what is going on and why things happen you need information. Often teachers and other people give you the information you need for a specific lesson or activity and this book will give you some information too. But you cannot rely on this for everything; sometimes you have to use other sources of information to find out all the details you want to know about a subject. We can get this information from many different sources.

Local library
Librarians can help you find the right book for any topic. You can also order books from other libraries.

School library
You may be able to find books on topics covered in other lessons.

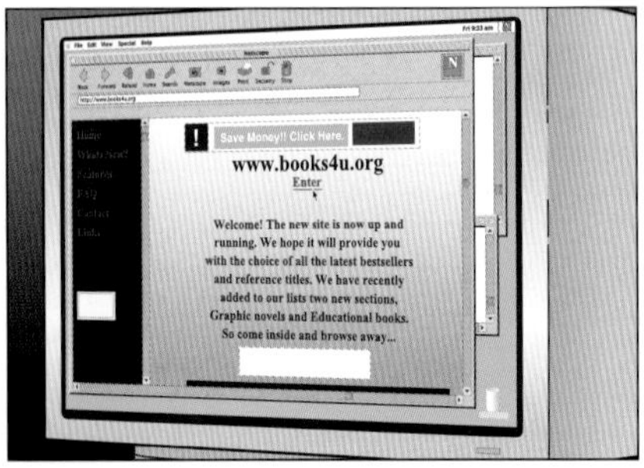

The internet
This can really speed things up. You can get information from the county council and government much more easily than waiting for the post.

Other people
Most people can tell you about where they live, what they have experienced and how they see things changing. Many people will have specialist knowledge to help you with special topics.

Television
News can be a good source of information. Other programmes can also give you a more detailed view of events or issues.

Posters
Some posters are designed to convince you to buy something but others are to provide information. Can you think of any examples?

Specialist organisations
Many organisations have lots of experience in one particular area: for example, 'Kick Racism Out Of Football' have information on anti-racism and football. You could write to these organisations to ask for leaflets and reports.

TASKS

1 What sources of information are missing from the list?

2 Can you think of an advantage and a disadvantage of each of the sources of information?

3 On the next page is a list of people who are preparing for a Citizenship project. Read the descriptions of what they are doing and advise them on the best sources of information they could use for their work.

What information do these people need?

Jack
He is planning his project on bullying. He wants to find out why people bully and how much bullying goes on in his school. He is also interested in finding out what other schools in the area do to see if there are other approaches to dealing with bullying.

Natasha
She wants to do her project on the housing estates where she lives. They are quite run down at the moment but the council is talking about improving the area. She wants to know why the tall blocks of flats were built in the first place and how her family can try to have a say in the plans for the area.

Michael
He wants to do his project on the local expanding football club. They have plans for redeveloping their grounds and increasing the capacity. He wants to know why the club wants to do this and also who they have to convince to get permission to rebuild the stadium.

Foyzul
He is planning a project on local environmental issues. He wants to find out what happens to all of the rubbish that is collected in the local area. He also wants to know what alternatives there are for getting rid of rubbish, how it can be recycled and who can help.

Adile
She is interested in the local area. She wants to look at how it has changed over time and what it might be like in the future. She is particularly interested in the range of different cultures in the area. She needs to know when certain groups arrived in the area, where they came from, where their descendants live and which new groups are arriving now. She would also like to find out how the area has been changed by the range of people there now.

Marian
She enjoys watching *The Bill* on television. She wants to know how realistic it is and to find out more about her local police service. She also needs to find out how the police are run, who tells them what to do and what differences there are between local areas.

KEEPING TRACK

As you work through this book and other Citizenship activities keep a record of what sources of information you use. Draw a table with all the sources of information down one side, and leave space next to it to record when you used that source and what you used it for.

Source	Date	What it was used for
Local library		
Internet		

Developing opinions

Why should you be good?
What is good behaviour?
Who should decide whether you are being good or not?

These are the kinds of questions that can keep you talking for a long time. There are some things that we just cannot agree about. But many things we disagree about keep us talking anyway because they are important. Sometimes we just want to show people the reasons why we think the way we do. At other times we want to convince others that they should agree with us. Whether we are telling someone about ourselves, or trying to bring them around to our way of thinking, we have to tell them what we think and why we think it.

TASKS

Make a pair with someone else in the class and look at the following examples of people who need to explain themselves.

1 Choose one example and pick one character each to think about. Write down some of the things they might say to let the other person know what their opinion is.

2 Now write down some of the reasons they might have to support their opinion.

3 Now compare your answers with your partner. Between you, write a conversation the characters might have. Make sure you come up with clear examples to support each character's opinion.

4 Read the conversation through to make sure it makes sense and then present it to the rest of the class.

5 Give some positive feedback to people as they make their presentations. Try to focus on how good they were at giving reasons for their opinions. After your presentation, make a note of the feedback you got from others in the class. See if you can improve the work.

6 Did any of the pairs come to an agreement through their conversation? Do you think any of them could agree with each other? What suggestions could you make to help them now that you have heard their reasons?

▼ Situation A – Bob and Barbara

Situation B – Ahmed and Ahmed's Mum

Situation C – Cynthia and Auntie Doreen

Situation D – Phil and Phil's Dad

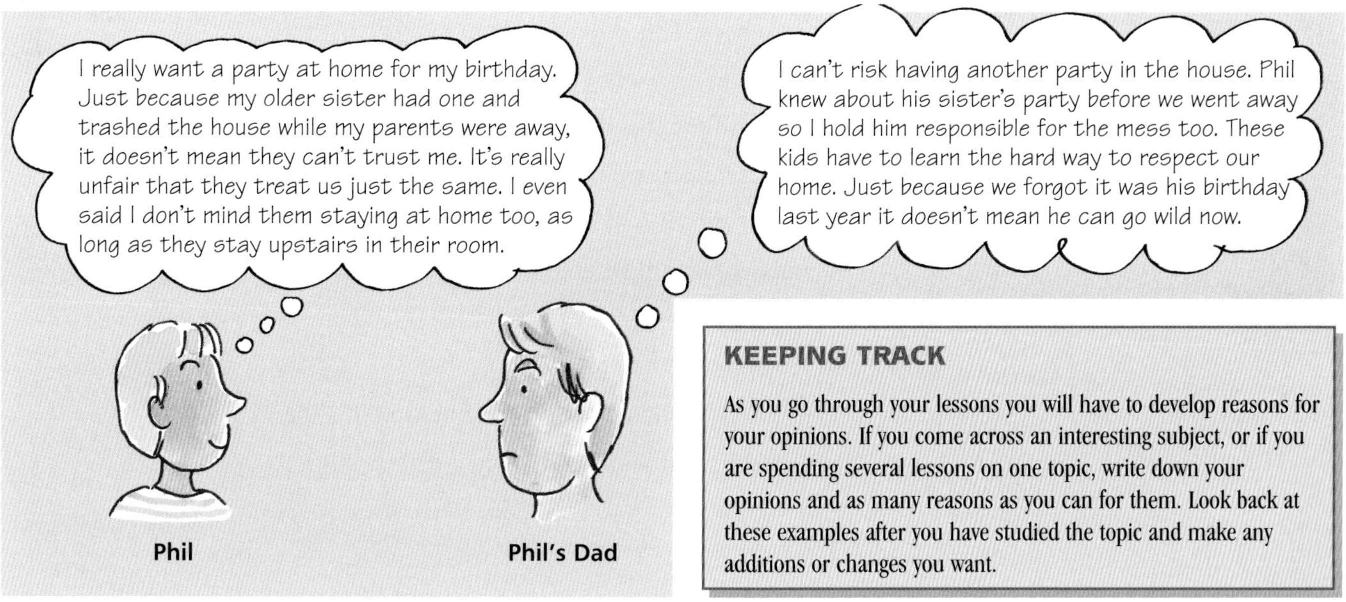

KEEPING TRACK

As you go through your lessons you will have to develop reasons for your opinions. If you come across an interesting subject, or if you are spending several lessons on one topic, write down your opinions and as many reasons as you can for them. Look back at these examples after you have studied the topic and make any additions or changes you want.

Debate and discussion

Issue: School Uniform

Motion: We Support Compulsory School Uniform

Jane's class is going to have a debate about whether everyone should have to wear a school uniform. Her teacher has split the class in two. Half have been asked to disagree with the motion, arguing that every student should not be forced to wear a uniform. Jane's half of the class are supporting the motion, and will have to argue that students should wear a uniform.

Once she had written her first draft she showed it to someone else on her team. They made comments around the page. Would you have any more comments to make on Jane's first draft?

Planning for a debate

Jane started by writing a list of points she could make for the motion. The list is started below:

Points in favour of the motion

1. *Everyone will feel as if they 'belong' together if they dress the same way.*
2. *It makes school feel completely different to outside life. This will make school more like a place you go to work, and help to make it better.*

Can you think of any other arguments Jane could add to her list?

From this list, Jane picked her top three points for the speech. Look at her first draft and say whether you think she has chosen the best points.

Jane's speech – first draft

No introduction

My first point is that they are a good thing because students will not make horrible comments about what other people are wearing if we all wear the same thing.

What does this refer to?

Can we add to this to make it stronger?

My second point is that they are a good thing because keeping up with the fashion costs a lot of money. Not everyone has enough money to have lots of clothes. School uniform would mean that everyone has to buy fewer clothes for school. This will save them money.

Repeating the same phrase

It also means nice clothes last longer

My third point is that they are a good thing because everyone is easy to spot. If we go on school trips it will be easy to stay together, and people will be able to know where we come from.

Also means 'trouble-makers' can be identified on the bus to school.

I think you should vote for the motion, it's the best solution.

This conclusion needs improving. Try to sum up the main points in a few words.

Jane's class has drawn up some rules for the debate. Each time someone does one of the following they gain one point:

- make a point clearly
- explain your point
- have a good introduction that says what you are arguing for
- finish with a summary and conclusion
- speak clearly and look at people as you speak.

They have also agreed that people should lose a point if they do any of the following:

- speak when someone else is speaking
- try to talk before it is your turn.

TASKS

1 Write a second draft of Jane's speech. Go through and decide how many points she already has.

2 Compare your answer with someone else in the class. Can you agree how many points the speech is worth?

3 Jane will get more points if she presents the speech well. Practise Jane's speech yourself and ask someone else in the class to award you marks for your presentation. You could also make the speech to the class and see how many extra points you can get.

An Argument Against Uniforms

Exclusion threat to poor pupils not in uniform

A report, 'Uniform Failure', has called on the government to order councils to provide school uniform grants for low-income families.

Of 125 local education authorities surveyed, 36 did not provide any financial help, it said. Only 49 provided help at both primary and secondary school level.

'Not having the proper uniform can mark out a child as being poor or even as being a troublemaker', said David Harker, chief executive of the National Association of Citizens' Advice Bureaux.

Uniform costs ranged from £105 to £274, but the average grant available when a child started secondary school was £49, the report said.

From *The Guardian*, 11 January 2001, by Will Woodward

HELPFUL HINTS

Sentence starters:

Introduction

I am going to argue that ...

I support the idea that ...

The Argument

One reason for this view is ...

This is important because ...

One of the main arguments in favour of this view is ...

Another supporting piece of evidence is ...

Finally ...

Conclusion

To summarise ...

You should support my view because ...

In conclusion ...

TASKS

Imagine you are in the other half of Jane's class. You will have to argue against the motion and say that uniforms are a bad idea.

1 Read the extract 'Exclusion threat to poor pupils not in uniform'. This should help you start a list of points arguing against uniforms. Add in your own ideas too.

2 Look through your list and choose the top three points for your speech.

3 Write your first draft of a speech. The Helpful Hints box might be useful.

4 Once you have read through your first draft, ask someone else to check it through and comment on it.

5 If you need to, write a second draft of your speech.

6 Practise the speech and present it to someone else in the class. Ask them to mark your speech for you. Discuss the points they gave you – do you agree?

7 You could present the best ones to the whole class and talk about what people have done which helped them to get most points.

8 Why not have your own debate? Pick a topic to interest the class and split into two teams. Agree the rules you want to follow and take it in turns to make your speeches.

KEEPING TRACK

Debating involves a number of skills. It will be useful to keep track of how you are doing in debates as you go through the course. Write down what you found easy and what you found most difficult.

Getting involved

Playing a part around the school

There are lots of opportunities for you to get involved in school activities. These give you the chance to:

- **help other people**
- **work with others to make changes happen**
- **contribute to making the school a better place**
- **solve problems**
- **represent the school**
- **help make decisions.**

Look at the following examples of active citizenship in schools:

A Mohammed
Mohammed was elected by the other students in his class. He represents the views of other students and helps to make decisions in the school. He sometimes gives up some of his own time for such activities.

L Cathy
Cathy is very helpful when the class is doing group work. She always makes sure that people are ready to do their presentations on time and also gets everyone involved.

K Sonia
Sonia has agreed to help Milena, who is new to the class and to the country. Sonia will help her with her new timetable, take her to class and look after her during break time.

B Mandy
Mandy voted for Mohammed to be her representative. She had to decide between three of her friends but voted for Mohammed in the end because he is the best listener.

▼ Active citizens

J Everyone
The whole school celebrates Red Nose Day by having a non-uniform day. Everyone has to donate 50p for not wearing their uniform and it all goes to charity.

TASKS

1. Which activities do you think are the easiest to do, and which are the most difficult? List the examples in order.
2. Which of these activities are going on in your school?
3. What else is happening in your class or school that shows young people being actively involved in running things?
4. Pick one of the activities and describe the skills the person would need to do it well.
5. What activities have you been involved in through school?
6. What skills did you use in those activities?

C Bill and Jane
They give up some of their time and effort helping the class run smoothly. This can involve helping to lay the room out correctly at break time, giving out and collecting equipment, keeping records of house points or merit marks for their tutor group.

D Mike
Mike enjoys swimming and did a sponsored swim for a national charity. He raised money from staff and students at school, as well as friends and neighbours near his home. He sent the money to the charity, which collected over £100,000 in total.

E Class 7G
All the students in 7G had lessons in storytelling from a professional storyteller. Once they had practised they went to a local primary school to tell stories and play games with younger students. They passed on some of their skills.

F John
John is a brilliant football player and trains at his local club at weekends. He works with the PE teacher to coach the younger students in the evenings.

G Amina
Amina is a peer counsellor. When friends have had arguments and they are not getting along they can go to Amina or one of the other counsellors to try to work things out. She had to train for her position in her own time and gives up break times to meet with people.

H Barry
Barry is a keen gardener. He worked with a gardening group in his primary school and started up his own gardening club in his new secondary school. He worked with teachers to get the money for equipment and has got a group of 15 students together to improve the school garden.

I Lucy
Lucy collects crisp packets and drinks cans for the school. She trades the crisp packets for books for the library and the drinks cans are sent for recycling.

7 What would a school be like where no one did any of these activities?

8 What new activity would you like to happen in your school? This can be from the list here or another activity you have thought of.

9 What new activity would you like to get involved in?

10 What would you need to help you take part in that new activity?

KEEPING TRACK

Once you have learned what is going on in your school, it should be easier for you to get involved and to help to make a change for the better. This could be any of the activities above and many more. Every term try to think of one activity you could do as part of your work or in your spare time which would help others, show you can work together with others or contribute to a group goal. Keep records of what you have achieved and try to think about how you are getting better as you get more practice.

Wants and needs

What is the difference between wants and needs? Have you ever thought about what you need to survive and grow up healthily? These are some rights all children are entitled to. They are different from just wanting things.

SKILLS FOCUS

- Seeing situations from other people's point of view
- Solving problems and **resolving** conflict

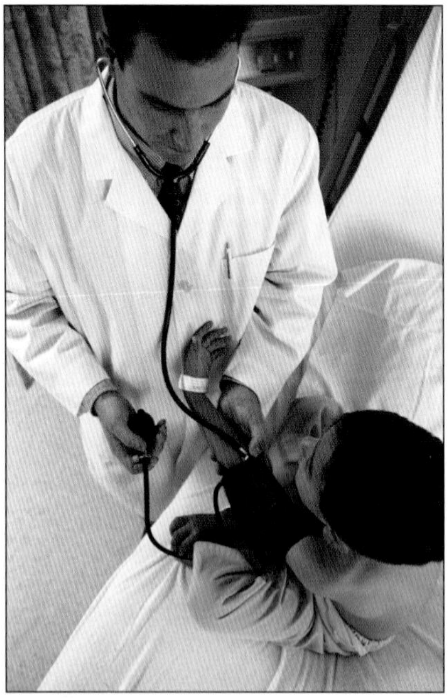

▲ Medical care when you need it

▲ Nutritious food

▲ Clean water

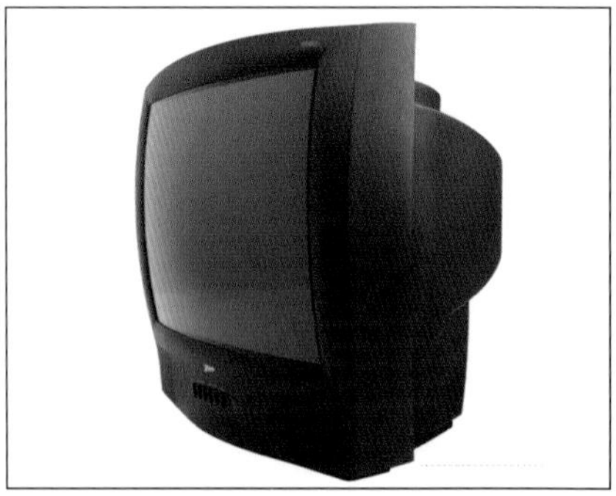

▲ TV

▲ Education

USEFUL WORDS

Convention – An agreement between several countries

Resolve – Solve a problem or sort out a difficult situation by reaching agreement

Violate – Break someone else's rights

Court injunction – An instruction from the court to stop doing something

▲ Your own bedroom

Being able to express your opinion and be listened to

Clean air

Decent shelter

Holidays

Playgrounds and leisure centres

Fashionable clothes

TASKS

1 Are there any items that you feel are important for a good life but are missing from these pages? Can you add another 5?

2 Imagine only 12 items can be provided from the list, not 18. Which 6 items are you willing to give up? Give reasons for your choices.

3 Imagine another 6 items have to be cut from the list. Which ones are you going to get rid of this time?

4 Was it more difficult to cut the list down the second time than the first? Why?

5 Which items on the list are wants, and which ones are needs?

6 Do you think wants and needs are different for different people?

7 Which of the above do you think you should have a right to?

8 Draw up your own list of rights, that you consider basic for people of your age.

9 Now compare your list with the UN **Convention** on the Rights of the Child (you will find it on page 14). How similar or different is your list?

Whose right? Whose responsibility?

Children's basic rights are protected by the UN Convention on the Rights of the Child. This is an international law and all the countries of the world have agreed to make this law work, except two: the USA and Somalia. Your rights are about what you are allowed to do and what the people responsible for you are allowed to do. However, it is important to understand that having these rights brings responsibilities towards other children and adults. If we want to enjoy our rights we also have to make sure we respect everyone else's rights.

TASKS

1. Which Articles strike you as being the most important?
2. Are there any Articles you were not aware of in the Convention?
3. Select four Articles and think of a personal experience, or an event that you have heard about on the TV or radio or read about in newspapers, linked to your choice.
4. Prepare a 2-minute presentation on one of the Articles. In your presentation mention the following:
   - why you have chosen this Article
   - what it means to you personally
   - what responsibilities does this also give us in our relations with other young people?

UN Convention on the Rights of the Child

Article 1: A 'child' is every human being below the age of 18 years

Article 2: Every child has these rights regardless of race, colour, sex, language, religion, national, ethnic or social origin

Article 7: You have the right to a name, a nationality and the right to know and be cared for by your parents

Article 9: You should not be separated from your parents unless it is for your own good

Article 12: You have the right to give your opinion when a decision made by adults will affect you

Article 14: You have the right to think what you like and be whatever religion you want to be. Your parents should help you to learn what is right and wrong

Article 15: You have the right to meet, make friends and join clubs with other people, unless it interferes with the rights of others

Article 16: You have the right to a private life

Article 19: No one should hurt you in any way. Adults should make sure you are protected from abuse, violence and neglect. Even your parents have no right to hurt you

Article 22: If you are a refugee you have the right to special protection

Article 23: If you are disabled, either mentally or physically, you have the right to special care and education to help you grow in the same way as other children

Article 24: You have the right to good health. This means you should have professional care and medicines when you are sick

Article 27: You have the right to a good enough 'standard of living'. This means that parents have the responsibility to make sure you have food, clothes, a place to live, etc. If parents cannot afford this, the government should help

Article 28: You have a right to education. You must have primary education, and it must be free. You should also be able to go to secondary school

Article 31: You have the right to play and leisure

Article 32: You have the right to be protected from working in places or conditions that are likely to damage your health or get in the way of your education. If somebody is making money out of your work you should be paid fairly

Article 42: All adults and all children should know about the Convention. You have a right to learn about your rights and adults should learn about them too.

(Some articles have been left out – if you want to find the whole document you could visit the website www.unicef.org/crc)

Whose right? Whose responsibility?

Scenario 1: Sarah and Tom's dad has been unemployed for over six months, since the car factory he used to work in closed down. Their mum has got a part-time job in the local bakers, she does not get paid very much. The benefits the family receives and mum's salary are just enough to pay the bills and the rent. There is not enough money to buy the amount of food the family needs. Sarah and Tom do not have enough to eat, they are small for their age and are not doing well at school.

Scenario 2: Aisha is 13 years old. As part of her religious beliefs she has to start wearing a hejab (headscarf) and shalwar (trousers) to school so her body is covered. She is the only girl dressed like this at her school. The headmistress has told her that she is not allowed to wear these items and that she must wear school uniform. Her parents do not agree with the headmistress, and so Aisha has been suspended from school.

Scenario 3: Francis is 11 and wants to start doing a paper round to earn some extra pocket money for a new electronic game. He would have to start work at 6am every morning. His parents think he is too young to do the job and are worried about his health and safety.

Scenario 4: Jack begged his parents for a pet dog and promised to look after it. Eventually his parents bought him one. For a year or so he looked after it well, taking it for walks and feeding it. However, recently he has been forgetting to do this. Jack's dad has had to do it. He keeps telling Jack off and has threatened to take the dog to Battersea dogs' home.

TASKS

1. Copy and complete the table.
2. With a partner, choose one of the scenarios and create a role play showing the problem and how it could be resolved. In your speeches make sure you include the rights and responsibilities of the people involved.
3. What have you learnt about rights and responsibilities from the scenarios?
4. Write a speech about rights and responsibilities. Try to use examples to back up your points. You could perhaps make your speech amusing or base it on instructing younger children that children's rights do not mean that you have everything your own way.

What is the problem?	Who is responsible for solving the problem?	How could the problem be **resolved**?	Is this a problem about wants or rights?

Rights and responsibilities in the local community

Your local community is not just the area where you live. In your local community people have things in common and there are certain areas of life that are shared by all local residents. In order for a community to run smoothly everybody has to play a part. People have to take responsibility for their community so that everybody can maintain their individual rights.

TASKS

1 Make a list of all the things that people living in the same community would share.

2 What rights do you think people should have in the local community?

We all have to take responsibility for our own environment. If people do not take responsibility then other people will suffer. This picture shows what happens if people do not behave responsibly about their rubbish.

TASKS

1 Describe what you can see in the picture.

2 How would you feel if you lived in the local area?

3 Who is not taking responsibility for their local community?

4 Who could help improve the situation?

5 Do you have any problem areas like this in your local area? If so, could you do anything about it? Would you do anything about it? Explain your answers.

Neighbours from hell

There are many examples of 'neighbours from hell' in both local and national newspapers and on the television. In some towns there are as many as one in eight council-home tenants making complaints about neighbours every year. The complaints are usually about seriously unacceptable behaviour, for example harassment because of a neighbour's different beliefs or background, violent and threatening behaviour, neighbours destroying other people's property, and noise. All these types of behaviour are not acceptable as they **violate** our rights.

TASKS

Imagine the worst possible neighbour you could have.

1 Draw a picture of your nightmare neighbour and their house.

2 Explain why they are a bad neighbour.

3 How are your rights being violated by them?

The problem of people not considering their neighbour's rights can become extremely serious. People often get the police involved, some people get **court injunctions** to stop a neighbour from repeating the unacceptable behaviour and sometimes the neighbours who are causing the problem can be evicted and have to move to a different area.

Noise is one of the biggest reasons why neighbours complain to the police or local council. The noise they complain about includes loud music and television, barking dogs, using noisy electrical equipment and noisy children. A recent survey suggested that 14 per cent of the adult population are bothered by the level of noise created by their neighbours. People can become extremely upset, especially if they are not sleeping because of the noise. If the problem is not tackled in the right way it can make enemies of neighbours.

TASKS

Imagine you had a neighbour who for the last week had been playing music throughout the night at a very loud volume. You live near them so are reluctant to upset them. Your local council noise-pollution department has suggested that you first talk to your neighbour yourself.

1 Plan when and what you will say to your neighbour.

2 Write a dialogue between you and your noisy neighbour based on:
- your neighbour being understanding about your concerns

or
- your neighbour being completely unreasonable about your concerns.

3 If your neighbour refuses to turn the music down what further steps could you take, perhaps with other local residents, to resolve the situation?

What is diversity?

We are all similar to each other in many ways. We also have many differences that make us special individuals. The questions below will help you find out about some of the similarities and differences between people in your class.

Copy the following questions onto a sheet of paper, then make up your own questions for 7, 8 and 9 and write them into the boxes on the bottom line. Find examples from the class to write in each box. If there is no one in your class to answer a box, try to think who else in your school, or in your local community, you could ask.

1 Who in your class was born outside the UK?	**2** Who speaks a second language at home or with friends?	**3** Who has been on holiday to Europe, Asia or Africa?
4 Who can name a football team from another country?	**5** Who can name a food from the Caribbean, Italy or China?	**6** Who has visited places of worship from more than one religion?
7 ?	**8** ?	**9** ?

SKILLS FOCUS

- Think about the actions you can take to support equal opportunities
- Research equal opportunities in your school

Respecting differences

Some people face **discrimination** because of these differences. **Equal opportunities** means giving everyone the same chance to build a good life for themselves, regardless of their differences. Everyone has a part to play in this, and all of us can help achieve equal opportunities by challenging discrimination.

"*It is our different backgrounds that separate us and by bringing children together in the classroom we lay the foundations for a better future for all children in the country.*"
Doreen Lawrence, speaking after the racially motivated murder of her son, Stephen

USEFUL WORDS

Discrimination – Behaving differently towards people because they are different to you in some way

Equal opportunities – Everyone has the same chance of achieving success

Diversity – The differences between us

Inclusive – Accepting everyone's differences and trying to provide equal opportunities

The rest of this chapter will help you think about two equal opportunities issues – gender and disability.

TASKS

1. What similarities do you share with your classmates?
2. What differences are there between you and your classmates?
3. How important are these differences and similarities between you?

Plashet School

Background information

Plashet is a girls' secondary school in the heart of the East End of London. The majority of its students come from Pakistani, Bangladeshi and Indian communities.

Equal opportunities summary

We value our **diversity** and recognise the contribution it makes to our lives and education.

As a school we have a responsibility to:
- promote the benefits of diversity in a multicultural and multilingual society
- promote equality
- oppose any form of discrimination towards particular groups or individuals.

Aims

Our aims are to:
- ensure that everyone has opportunities to succeed in lessons
- ensure a safe environment for everyone in school
- encourage students to develop positive identities
- reflect the diversity of the students in what we do in school
- promote understanding and respect for each other
- challenge discrimination
- equip students with the skills for life
- welcome parents to contribute to the life of the school.

Action 1 – Students

Celebrating International Women's day by making and selling ribbons. Decorating the evergreen oak with mobiles highlighting the names of famous women, the role of women throughout the world, and women's movements working for social justice.

Action 2 – Teachers

Being aware and preparing suitable material for pupils with special needs – for example, those with English as a second language, or students with specific learning difficulties, such as visual impairment and Down's Syndrome.

Action 3 – Parents

Parents attend Year Six induction interviews with their child. They agree to sign and honour the school's 'code of conduct' policy.

Action 4 – Support staff

Actively encouraging pupils with special educational needs to be part of everyday school routines such as joining extra-curricular activities and following similar timetables to the rest of their form group.

TASKS

Look at the Plashet School case study above.

1 Do you agree with the equal opportunities policy?

2 Which parts do you think are the most important? Give reasons.

3 Who needs to know about the school's equal opportunities policy?

4 How can all these people find out about it?

5 Who do you think should be involved in writing a policy like this?

6 What should the following groups do to make the policy work?

(a) Teachers
(b) Students
(c) Senior management
(d) Support staff including office staff and lunch supervisors
(e) Governors
(f) Parents

Can anyone else help the school make its policy work?

7 Write your own case study for your school. Use the same headings as the one above.

TAKING IT FURTHER

You could do a project on your School's equal opportunities policy. Think about the following questions:

How was your school policy written?
- Who was involved?
- When was it written?
- Has it been revised since it was written?

How aware are people of the policy?
- Carry out a survey to find out whether or not people know about the school's policy.
- Plan a campaign to tell people more about it.
- Do people agree with the policy?
- Organise a debate about what should happen in the future.

Focus on gender

▲ Do women do more work than men?

TASKS

1 What jobs is the woman juggling?

2 Which of these is she paid for?

3 (a) Describe what needs to be done for each of the jobs.

(b) How long do you think each job takes per week?

4 How much would each job cost if you had to pay someone to do it? (Check what the minimum wage is.)

5 How much would she earn if she were paid a fair wage for doing all the work?

6 Who does this work in your home?

7 How many of the tasks are shared out in your home?

8 Compare your answers to those of others in the class. Is it mainly women who do this work or are things changing?

9 Draw a similar picture for a man.

10 Are there still big differences between women's and men's work?

What message is the poster trying to get across?

Throughout history women and men have often done the same kinds of work. However, women's work often is not valued as highly as that of men. In many ways opportunities are improving for women, but nevertheless, women are still campaigning to have equal standing in the workplace.

Look at the following information. Why do such differences still exist? What could be done to ensure equality?

Facts and figures (the figures given below refer to pay per hour)

Full-time employee earnings in April 1999

£10.75 for men £8.70 for women

Part-time employee earnings in April 1999

£7.41 for men £6.45 for women

Pay in education (average pay per hour)

	Men	Women
Professional jobs	£15.40	£13.90
Administrators	£14.10	£11.70
Secretarial	£7.90	£6.80

Health and social work
(average pay per hour)

	Men	Women
Professional jobs	£17.90	£13.20
Administrators	£15.00	£11.10
Secretarial	£7.60	£6.40
Nurses	£10.10	£9.70
Manual jobs	£5.40	£4.50

Banking, insurance and pension funding

	Men	Women
Professional jobs	£23.70	£14.70
Bank managers	£19.10	£12.70
Secretarial	£8.70	£8.00

80% of employees in health and social work are women

75% of employees in education are women

52% of employees in banking, insurance and pension funding are women

However, the majority of women in these fields work in secretarial jobs whereas the majority of men work as managers.

Disability

What is disability?

What immediately springs to mind when you hear the word 'disability'? For many people a picture of a wheelchair is one of the first images that they think of. While it is true that some disabled people are in wheelchairs, the word 'disability' has a far broader meaning.

Being disabled should not limit people's use of services. Schools can play an important part in helping to ensure equal opportunities for young people with disabilities. One example in education is people who are dyslexic. Dyslexia is a condition also known as 'word blindness'. It means that people have difficulty in reading and spelling. It does not affect the intelligence of an individual, but it is a very frustrating condition to have as it makes written communication difficult. A dyslexic student often receives additional individual help from support teachers and through access to computers.

Case study: Boy with Diabetes Banned From School Trips

Around 1.4 million people in the UK have diagnosed diabetes. Diabetes is a disease of the pancreas that prevents the body from absorbing sugar and starch properly. In many cases, the disease can be controlled by insulin injections and patients can lead a normal life. In the UK, there are over 20,000 young people under the age of 20 with diabetes.

A Lancashire school which has banned a 15-year-old boy from going on school trips because he has diabetes is being taken to court by the Disability Rights Commission. This is the first court case taken against a school under the Disability Discrimination Act 1995.

Tom White has been banned from school trips by Clitheroe Royal Grammar School because he had his first severe hypoglycaemic attack while on a skiing trip last February. The school then ruled that Tom would not be able to take part in a watersports trip to France next year.

Tom, a keen sportsman, has managed his diabetes for many years and this was the first blackout he has ever had.

The ban not only affects Tom's ability to take part in leisure activities through the school; he was recently stopped from going on a trip to Germany. Tom is studying GCSE German. The Disability Rights Commission is taking Tom's case to court because the school has discriminated against him because of his disability.

Malcolm White, Tom's father, said, 'Tom is devastated by the ban. It is totally unfair to stop him from going on trips with his friends and other pupils just because he has diabetes. We have tried every channel to get the school to change their minds but they have chosen to ignore the medical, educational and legal experts.'

TASKS

1 How would you feel if you were Tom?

2 How would you feel if Tom was on a school trip with you?

3 Do you think Tom should be allowed to go on school trips?

4 What precautions could be taken so that Tom would not be discriminated against in the future?

Disability Discrimination Act 1995

Since December 1996, it has been illegal to treat disabled people less favourably than other people because of their disability. Since October 1999, businesses and organisations have been required to introduce reasonable measures for the employment of disabled people, such as providing extra help in the workplace or changing the way they provide their services. In addition, schools, colleges, and universities have to provide information about their facilities for disabled students and the government sets minimum standards in public-transport systems to assist disabled people in using trains and buses etc.

ACTIVITY: Interior designer

You are an interior designer employed by the Feng Shui Secondary School. The school has recently introduced an **Inclusive** Learning policy. This means that all young people, regardless of any disability, have a right to learn there. Unfortunately, the classrooms are not 'wheelchair friendly'.

You have been asked to redesign the classrooms, to ensure that they are in line with the Inclusive Learning policy.

1. Draw a plan for the classroom as it is, based on the note about classroom layout on the right.
2. Label the problems.
3. You may decide to add other problems with your own school buildings.
4. Now redraw your design of the room. It must be wheelchair accessible and hold 30 students in total.
5. Label the changes you have made. You may like to use a colour-coding key, to make your ideas clearer.
6. Explain your changes. Write an evaluation justifying your decisions and the alterations you have made.
7. Swap designs with someone else and write a review on their design. Try to make positive comments about what they have changed and to suggest what further improvements could be made.

Note on classroom layout

- The classroom is accessible from the playground and corridor but there are four steps leading to each door.
- Double desks are arranged in rows in the class. There is limited space between aisles.
- The computers are situated in the corner of the class and are not easily accessible.
- The bookshelf runs from the floor to the ceiling. It is too high.
- The teacher's desk and chair are situated on a raised platform 30cm in height.

Overall, the classroom is cluttered and is not inviting to any learner, least of all those in wheelchairs.

Funding education – Who buys the pencils?

SKILLS FOCUS

- Use information to make decisions
- Justify decisions
- Think about the impact of decisions

USEFUL WORDS

Treasury – The government department that collects taxes and decides what services the money gets spent on

Local Education Authority (LEA) – The LEA shares out the money from government to schools and helps schools

Budget – The amount of money available to spend over a given period of time

Education Action Zone (EAZ) – Areas where achievement is low can get extra money for their schools if they become an EAZ

Who pays for your education? Who decides who gets what? Who decides what to spend the money on?

Schools are free to everyone in the country. But of course, although you and your parents do not pay when you attend school, this does not mean that schools are free to run. They require large amounts of money. Think about all the things a school needs to spend money on just to open every day.

The government raises money from people and businesses through tax. This money is spent by the **Treasury** on a number of services such as education. Can you think of other services the government provides with tax money?

The Department for Education and Skills (DfES) spent £41 billion in 1999, much of it on education. Most of the money passes from the government to local areas through **local education authorities**. These authorities then pass on about 80 per cent of the money to schools. The 20 per cent kept by local education authorities is spent on a number of services (these are described in the chapter on Democracy) and also pays for the salaries of inspectors and advisers who check what schools are doing and help them succeed.

The 80 per cent of the money passed on by the LEAs to schools is spent on delivering education for you. This includes wages for teachers and other staff, equipment such as computers and books, and maintenance of the buildings and grounds. Once all these things have been paid for, often there is not much left over for other areas the school might like to develop, such as new buildings.

TASKS

1. Copy the diagram on page 25 onto a sheet of paper.
2. Write in information against each of the arrows, showing what else the money is spent on.
3. Add any other information you can about how much money passes through at each stage.

Funding education – Who buys the pencils?

Citizens → **Private Schools**
Parents pay fees directly

↓ £ £ £ £ £ £ £

The Treasury
Collects money and decides how much money each government department gets to spend

↓ £ £ £ £ £ £ £

Department for Education and Skills

↓ £ £ £ £ £ £ £

Local Education Authorities

↓ £ £ £ £ £ £ £

Schools

Activity 1: Managing a budget

Introduction

Schools have some control over their budgets but there are limits within which they have to work. Most of the decisions about the money they have to spend are out of their control. This activity is about where the money comes from and the decisions headteachers and governors have to make about how it is spent.

The school you are representing has 7 forms in each year and each form has up to 30 students. For next year, years 8 to 11 are full, which gives you a total of 7 (forms) x 30 (students) x 4 (years) = ...?

For each student the school receives £2,730. Work out how much money the school already has and use this as the starting point for your score card.

INSTRUCTIONS

What you will need:

1 Copy the score card below. You will need this to record what happens in each round.

2 You will need a dice or 6 cards numbered 1 to 6.

How to play:

1 Get into groups of 4 to 6.

2 For each round, each person takes a turn to roll the dice or select a numbered card.

3 The number you get will match a box on page 27. This describes what happens to you. You must write down what happened and also how much you gain for each round on your score card.

4 When everyone in your group has completed round 1, 'Numbers of students in the new Year 7', then you repeat the instructions for round 2, and so on. Keep a running total in the column on the right of the score card.

5 When you get to round 6 you must remember the numbers have to be subtracted from the running total.

6 At the end of round 6 you will have your final budget for the year.

You can then turn to page 28 and begin Activity 2.

SCORE CARD — Starting point £...

Round	What happened?	Total
1		
2		
3		
4		
5		
6		

ROUND	1	2	3	4	5	6
Round 1: Numbers of students in the new Year 7	You have a waiting list 210 students £573,300	You are full 210 students £573,300	You are 5 students short 205 students £559,650	You are 10 students short 200 students £546,000	You are 20 students short 190 students £518,700	You are a whole class short 180 students £491,400
Round 2: Number of children with Statements of Special Needs	None x £4,000 £0	5 x £4,000 £20,000	15 x £4,000 £60,000	20 x £4,000 £80,000	30 x £4,000 £120,000	35 x £4,000 £140,000
Round 3: Education Action Zone	You are not part of an EAZ £0	You are not part of an EAZ £0	You are not part of an EAZ £0	You have joined together with local primary schools to form a mini-EAZ £20,000	You are part of an EAZ but have not organised your plans effectively £25,000	You are part of an EAZ and have several projects £70,000
Round 4: Other new money	You are piloting a literacy project £5,000	You are piloting a numeracy project £3,000	You have a grant to build a new IT centre £25,000	You have a grant to build a new sports centre £50,000	You are a beacon school £10,000	You have no new projects £0
Round 5: Income earned on the school site	A new phone mast is built in school £3,000	Your classes are used by an evening school £3,000	Your sports hall is used as part of the local sports-centre facilities £3,000	You have advertising on the school premises £1,500	Your premises make no extra money £0	Your premises make no extra money £0
Round 6: Last-minute costs	The canteen roof collapses Replacement: £20,000	Your IT server blows up Replacement: £5,000	School is vandalised New windows and clean up: £5,000	Smokers set a toilet on fire Replacement: £8,000	No emergency repairs £0	No emergency repairs £0

Activity 2: Planning your spending

You should have a figure now for your budget for the year. This activity will help you think about what the school might do with the money if you have plenty in your budget, or how it might make savings if you need to.

The following offer some suggestions about how you might save money. Think carefully about these choices.

Rank them in the order you would be likely to use them, put the worst option last.

1 Sell the playing fields Earn an extra £20,000	**2** Sack a teacher Save an extra £30,000	**3** Cut back on support staff Save an extra £15,000
4 Do not redecorate the old block Save an extra £10,000	**5** Scrap after-school clubs and activities Save an extra £2,500	**6** Stop subsidising trips for poorer families Save an extra £5,000
7 Increase canteen charges by 10 per cent Earn an extra £3,000	**8** Cut back on the number of cleaners Save an extra £5,000	**9** Charge students for textbooks Earn an extra £15,000

Sometimes schools can decide to spend money on more projects. If you have extra money in your budget, you can decide what to spend it on. Here are a few ideas but add some more of your own if you wish.

1 A new networked IT room £50,000	**2** A minibus (including the running costs) £20,000	**3** Redecoration of the school hall £15,000

Activity 3: Managing your budget

In this activity you have to make decisions about how you will manage the school budget. You will have to take your final figure from page 27 as your starting point.

To deliver the same service as last year your school will need £3,000,000.

If your budget is less than this you will need to make some savings. There are ideas on page 28 for you to choose from.

If your budget is above this figure then you have more to spend on the projects you like.

Remember, if you decide there is something new your school should really try to spend money on, you can decide to make savings in other areas.

Decision	Justification	Running total

Copy the table above to record the decisions you make. For each one give reasons to justify your decision.

It is important to think about the impact the decisions might have. Choose the most important decision you have made and use it to complete the following flow chart. Think about the knock-on effects of your decision – it may have some unintended and surprising results.

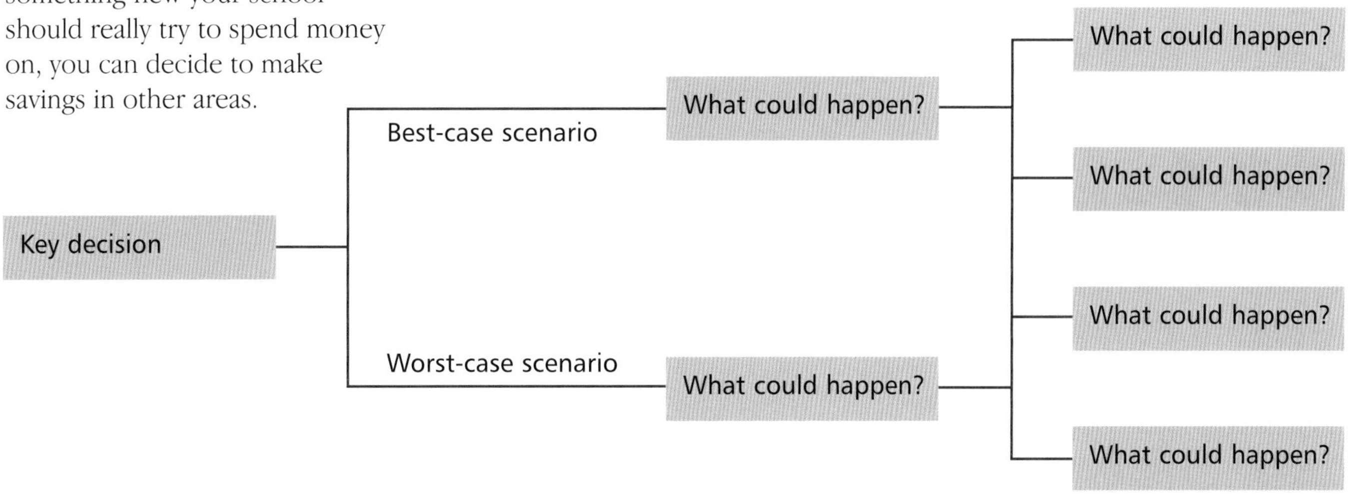

TASKS

1. What was the best thing to happen to you in Activity 1?
2. What was the worst thing to happen to you in Activity 1?
3. Did you have enough money to run the school?
4. What was the most important decision you had to make?
5. Did anyone in your group have worse problems than you?
6. Were there any surprises through the activities?
7. Did you have enough money to do all the things you wanted to?
8. What has this section told you about managing a school?

Democratic decision-making in everyday life

Lots of decisions are made in schools. Have you ever thought about who makes those decisions? Democratic decision-making means that all the people involved help make the decision.

Read through the following examples of how a decision was reached over school uniform. Say which ones are democratic. Are any more democratic than others?

a) The teachers had a meeting and decided that the new uniform will be a green and pink track suit.

b) The headteacher decided that everyone must wear a hat.

c) Every class elected someone to represent them at a meeting where uniform was discussed. The meeting agreed to introduce sandals during the summer term.

d) All students were asked their opinions. The five most popular changes were listed and every student voted for their preferred option. Shoes must now be polished every morning in registration.

e) Teachers asked their tutor groups what they wanted. They then met to discuss the options and the headteacher had the final say. Everyone now must wear a school blazer and tie.

In example (d) everyone had a **direct** say in what changes to the uniform should happen. In example (c) only elected representatives attended the meeting where the decision was made. In the UK we have a **representative democracy**. This means we choose the people to represent us and help to make decisions about how the government works. We do not have a vote on every decision the government makes for us.

USEFUL WORDS

Democracy – Government by the people

Direct democracy – People make decisions directly themselves

Representative democracy – People choose someone to represent them in government

SKILLS FOCUS

- Justify and discuss your opinions
- Decision-making

What kind of person makes a good representative?

Copy the diagram below and complete it by adding all the skills and qualities you would want in your representative.

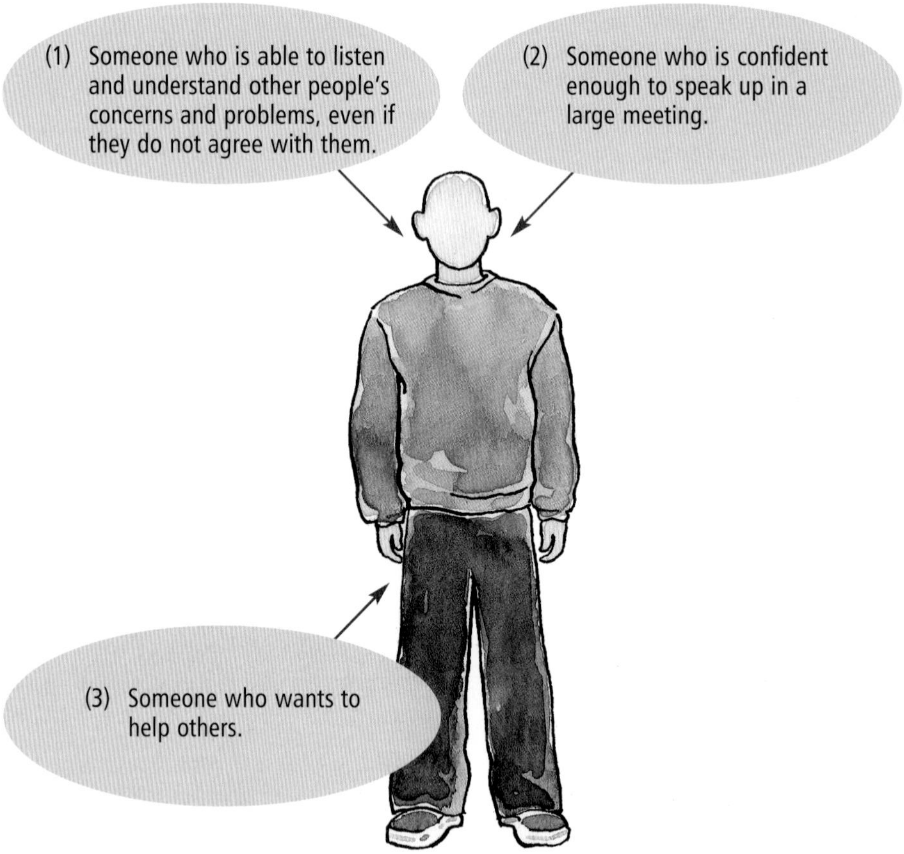

Do you think you would make a good student representative in your school?

Democracy in history

Democracy has had a long history and it has had many different meanings for many people. What we recognise as democracy today is not the same as what people in the past have understood by the word. Thousands of years ago the Ancient Greeks used the word to mean 'rule by the people'. This meant everyone could have a say and a vote in all decisions (but women and slaves were not included). Today, democracy in the UK means that adults vote for the people who run the government. This section of the book will be examining democracy at work on a local level by investigating local government.

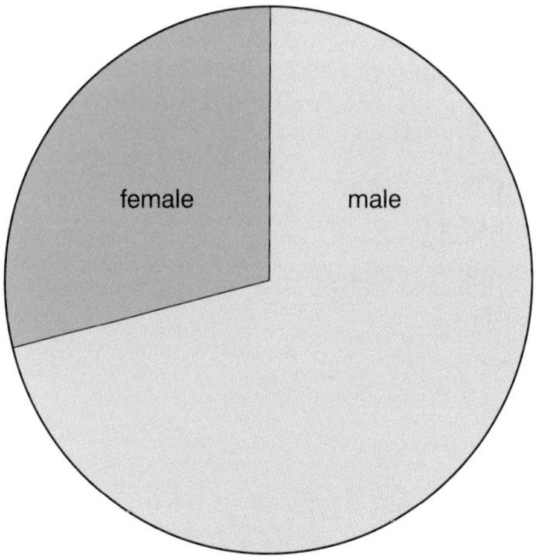

▲ Councillor's gender

Local government

Our representatives in local government are called councillors. Local government has a limited control over a limited area, usually a single town or county. Many of the decisions that seem most important are made at a national level. However, local government is in an excellent position to deal with the particular concerns and problems in a local area. This is largely because local councillors are people who live and work in the area that they represent. Such people are more likely to understand the issues that affect their own area and community. In other words they represent the interests of the local people.

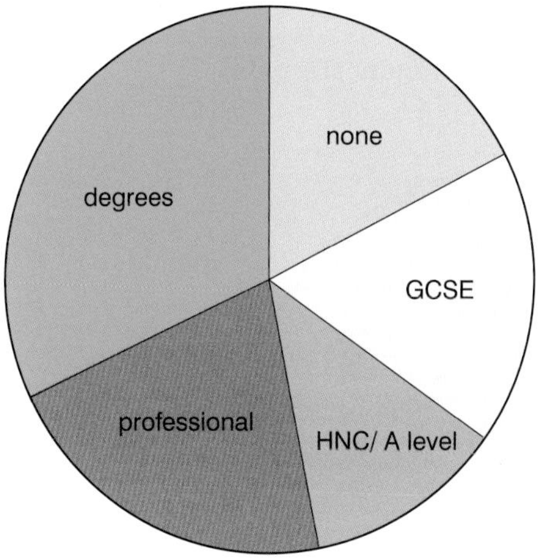

▲ Qualification of councillors

TASK

Read through the following statements and decide if they are true or false.

True False

1. Democracy means one person makes important decisions.
2. Democracy is a new idea.
3. Through history people have disagreed about what democracy means.
4. Councillors represent local residents.
5. Most councillors are female.
6. Councillors are the most powerful people in the country.
7. To be a councillor you must have been to university.
8. Every type of democracy requires representatives.
9. People always get what they want in a democracy.
10. In a democracy everyone can vote.

When you have completed the task, change all the false statements to make them into true statements. Write ten true statements about democracy into your notes.

What does the council do?

1. Education

Schools have a lot of power today to make their own decisions. But councils help schools by:

- providing training for teachers
- improving school buildings
- recruiting and training governors
- checking standards.

Councils also:

- provide adult education
- run the Youth Service
- provide nursery education
- provide support for pupils with Special Needs.

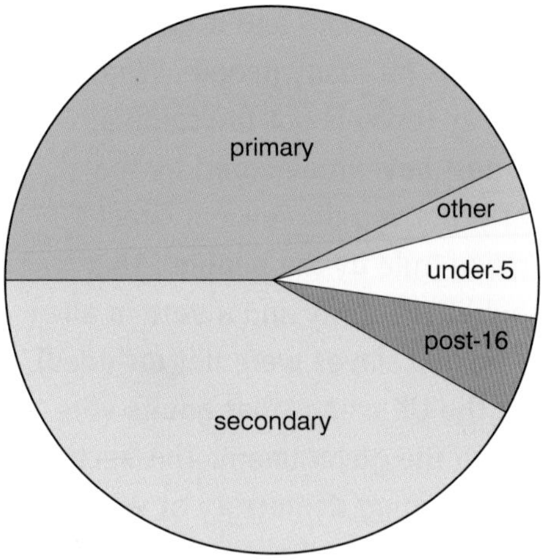

▲ How education budgets are spent

2. Social services

Councils have a very important role supporting people in need in the following ways:

- children in care (this affects 1 per cent of all children)
- organising and supporting foster care and adoption
- providing residential care for adults with disabilities
- supporting elderly people at home and in residential care (600,000 people).

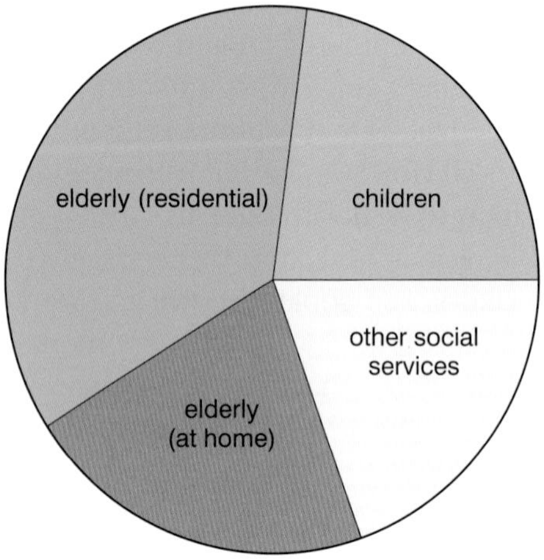

▲ How social services budgets are spent

3. Transport

Councils do not directly provide many transport services but they do monitor those provided by local companies. They also maintain 95 per cent of all roads, bridges and pavements.

4. Housing

Councils manage 3 million homes – that is 17 per cent of all homes in England and Wales. They are slowly passing on many council houses and flats to other landlords such as Housing Associations.

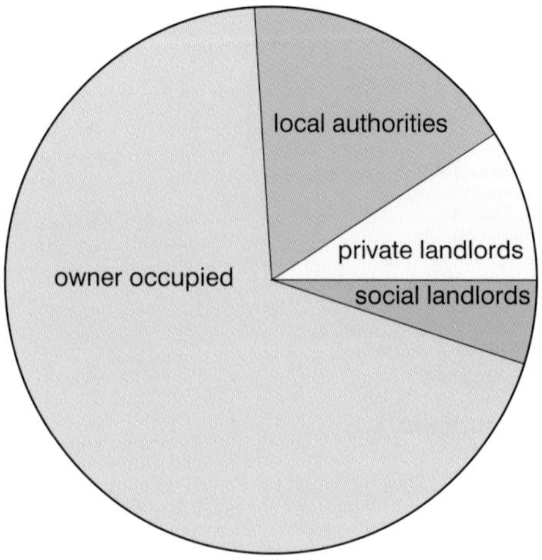

▲ Who owns our homes

5. Community safety

Councils have a number of roles to improve community safety:

- they run the fire service
- many councillors are part of independent police authorities
- councils can work with the police to take out anti-social behaviour orders against people who harass or harm other local people.

6. Environmental health

Councils carry out a number of activities to keep the local area healthy, such as:

- street cleaning
- keeping parks and open spaces
- food safety inspections in restaurants and other places
- rubbish collection
- Local Agenda 21 – Sustainable Development
- they are also in charge of local planning issues and make decisions about new building plans.

7. Leisure

Councils also provide services for local people to use in their spare time, including:

- libraries
- swimming pools and leisure centres
- supporting museums, galleries and theatres.

TASKS

1 Make a list under each of the 7 headings of any services you or your family have used.

2 Put each of the items in your list into the following table:

Service you can easily get somewhere else, without the council providing it	Service you may have gone without if the council did not provide it
Using a swimming pool	Using the local library

3 In the 1997 general election about 70 per cent of adults voted. In 2001 there was concern that the figure was closer to 60 per cent. But in local elections in 1999 only 30 per cent voted. Why do you think people are less likely to vote in local elections?

4 Local councils are trying to encourage more people to vote in local elections. Imagine you are trying to persuade people to turn out to vote in the next local election. You are in charge of a local campaign to try to encourage more people to vote. You can either have a poster campaign around your local area or post a leaflet to every house.

- Think about what services people would most value.
- Say why it is important for the services to continue.
- Think about how to make the council seem important to people's lives.
- Think about how to get your message across clearly.
- Say why it is important that people vote for their local council (think about local councillors' role as representative).

Difficult decisions

Most of the money councils spend comes from the taxes collected by central government. About 25 per cent is raised by local taxes. Councils have many difficult decisions to make in delivering all these services. When councillors set the budget for each year they have to discuss which areas are the most important to fund and which can make do with less money.

CASE STUDY:
Framptonshire County Council

400,000 people live in Framptonshire. In the year 2000–01, the council spent about £260 million, including the following:

	£
Education	150 million
Social services	45 million
Transport	15 million
Housing	10 million
Community safety	10 million
Environmental health	5 million
Leisure	10 million

This does not add up to the full budget as the council has other calls on its money over the course of a year – for example, Framptonshire also spent some money on countryside issues.

TASK

Imagine you are a councillor. You are about to meet to agree the final budget for your council. Choose one of the following projects to present to the meeting. In your presentation include the following:

- outline clearly what the proposal is
- explain who would benefit from the project
- explain why the project is a good idea
- explain why it is better than the other alternatives.

Project 1: Education

A local secondary school has almost no sports facilities. There is one large concrete playground and one smaller one. The smaller one has been unused for a while because the shelter covering the space is dangerous and has to be removed. The school could have a new series of sports halls, squash courts, pool and other gym equipment developed on this site. This would help the school to develop expertise in sports education and help it to deliver the national curriculum in PE properly.

Total cost: £1 million

Project 2: Social services

The council runs a children's home in a large old house in the countryside. There is already money in the budget to redecorate the old house (at a cost of £150,000). This project is the construction of a new home in the town, which will give the children easier access to their schools, shops and other leisure facilities.

Total cost: £1 million

Project 3: Transport

A local canal has been unused and full of rubbish for many years. This project would unblock the waterway and rebuild some of the locks. This will make the canal a more pleasant place for walking and fishing. It is also hoped that tourists will be attracted to the area and bring more money into the local economy in the long run.

Total cost: £1 million

Project 4: Housing

A tower block housing over 150 families is in desperate need of repair. This proposal will enable some of the worst flats to be renovated and all flats to be completely redecorated. It will also fund a landscaped garden around the block, rather than the wasteland that is there now. The outside of the block will be repainted to stop it looking so shabby.

Total cost: £1 million

Project 5: Community safety

A pilot project has just reported a great success on 'problem estates'. Private security guards have been patrolling one estate in the evenings and youth clubs have been set up. These measures cut crime during the year in which the project was running. The project is now seeking further money to keep operating and to expand its work to cover two other problem areas.

Total cost: £1 million

Project 6: Environmental health

At present, recycled waste is transported over 150 miles to the nearest recycling centre. Building a recycling plant in Framptonshire would both save on transport costs and reduce the pollution caused by the transport. In a survey local people identified recycling as one of their top 5 priorities.

Total cost: £1 million

Project 7: Leisure

There are a number of requests for funding which have been selected by the Leisure Committee for the council to consider:

- a local theatre will close next year unless it raises £500,000
- there are two school drama projects looking at drugs education and drama skills workshops; each requests £100,000 to run a 2-year project
- the local museum wants to boost the profile of Framptonshire by hosting an international art exhibition. It will cost £200,000
- ten community projects are hoping to run workshops and activity centres for families during the summer holiday. Each requests £10,000.

Total cost: £1 million

Community groups and clubs

Groups and clubs are very important to many people all over the world. They provide a place where we can meet people, learn skills and share interests. They are seen as so important that the right to join together in clubs has been included in the UN Convention on the Rights of the Child.

Read through the following examples and try to think of a suitable club or group the people could join.

SKILLS FOCUS

- Think about the skills you have
- Describe and teach your skills to others

Example 1

Tom loves music. He would really like the opportunity to create and mix his own music. The music teacher at school is very encouraging but the music department does not have the right equipment for the work he would like to do. There is not even an after-school music club because none of the teachers can stay late to supervise the group.

Example 2

Nisha is very adventurous. She would like to learn how to mountain climb and live outdoors. She wants to learn survival skills like being able to make a shelter and to identify wild plants that can be eaten.

Example 3

Joe and Holly live in a high-rise block of flats. They would both like to grow their own vegetables but they do not have a garden or the tools to be able to do this. They have never had a garden of their own and so have never developed gardening skills or practical knowledge.

Example 4

Jacob wants to be a nurse when he leaves school. He would like to find out what First Aid is all about. He would also be interested in having the opportunity to train other people.

USEFUL WORDS

Community group – Any group which brings people together voluntarily

Local Exchange Trade Schemes (LETS) – Local groups of people who exchange goods and services with each other for no money

TASKS

1 Where could the people in these examples find out about groups who could help them?

2 Do you know any local groups in your area that each of these people could join?

3 Are you, or any friends, a member of any local groups?

4 What local **community groups** do you know about? (Noticeboards are a useful source of information – check out local shop windows, places of worship and local newspapers for information about groups and clubs near you.)

5 Is each of your local groups aimed at specific people?

Local Exchange Trading Schemes (LETS)

Some community groups exist for people to come together because they share an interest or a particular need. How many local community groups can you think of which are like this?

Other groups, such as LETS, are more general and bring together people who have different skills and needs. LETS is a very simple idea that can make a big difference to people. It provides a way for local people to link with others in their area and exchange goods and services to help each other. No money changes hands, instead people swap whatever they can with each other to get what they want.

Case study:
Leighton Buzzard LETS and the buzzard

WORKING FOR LETSBUZZ LEIGHTON BUZZARD

In 1995 a group of people in Leighton Buzzard started their own LETS scheme. They decided to invent their own unit of currency, called the buzzard, so people could measure what they were exchanging without using real money. Scheme members advertise what they can offer in a local directory, and people contact them if they want to receive their service.

Example: If John teaches William how to design websites, they might agree that that service is worth 30 buzzards. This means John can use those buzzards to get a birthday cake from Alison, and William can design a website for Alison in exchange for two cakes (at 15 buzzards each).

The buzzards are not real money so no one needs to go to a bank or wait to be paid before they can get what they need. The system is based on trust because there are no banks to guarantee the buzzards. Also, as more people do more work for each other, the amount of buzzards will grow because the scheme members charge more to represent the job they are doing.

Service	Buzzards
Babysitting (one hour)	1
Baking a large cake	
Borrowing a computer game (1 week)	
Walking a dog (1 hour)	
Haircutting	
Helping with homework (2 hours)	
Washing a car	
Giving someone a lift in your car	
Cooking dinner	
Doing the washing up for a week	

TASKS

1. If one hour of babysitting is worth 1 buzzard, how many buzzards do you think the other services opposite are worth?
2. What are the advantages of LETS?
3. What could go wrong with LETS?
4. How might a LETS scheme help a community?
5. What skills could you offer a LETS scheme?

The Scouts

The Scouting movement is an incredibly successful community group. It has 25 million members worldwide. The rest of this section looks at this group's development, and considers what the Scouts do and why it has been such a popular organisation.

What is a Scout?

To 'scout around' means that someone is searching for something, or wishing to find out more. This is exactly what a Scout does.

In the military sense of the word, a scout is the person who goes in front of an army to find out where the enemies are, and what they are doing. The scout must then report back what he has discovered. In this situation, a scout must see, but not be seen; hear, but not be heard; follow, but not be followed.

How did it all start?

Robert Baden-Powell

Robert Stephenson Smyth Baden-Powell was born in London, England, on 22 February 1857. Baden-Powell and his four brothers loved the outdoor life. They went hiking and camping around many parts of England. When he was 19, Baden-Powell passed the army examinations and immediately accepted a chance to go to India.

The Boer War

In the Boer War (or South African Wars) (1880–1 and 1899–1902) Baden-Powell successfully led his army to defend the town of Mafeking for seven months. It was the first real victory of the Boer War, which eventually led to the re-establishment of British rule in South Africa.

Baden-Powell returned to England, a national hero. Already many young men and boys were reading his book *Aids to Scouting*. This book was originally intended as a military training-manual. On Baden-Powell's return, it was being used as a textbook in boys' schools.

Scouting for Boys

In the summer of 1907 Baden-Powell took a group of 20 boys with him to Brownsea Island in Poole Harbour for the first Boy Scout camp the world had ever seen. The camp was a great success. In 1908, Baden-Powell published his revised handbook for training, *Scouting for Boys*. It was published in six fortnightly parts, and was illustrated by Baden-Powell himself.

Originally the Scouting movement had been designed for boys. However, as early as 1909, Baden-Powell came across a number of girl-only troops – calling themselves Girl Scouts. The Girl-Guide movement was established in 1910 with the help of Baden-Powell's sister, Agnes. Later, his wife Olave became the leader of the Girl Guides.

Scout patrols and troops began to spring up – not just in England, but in numerous other countries as well. *Scouting for Boys* is now in fourth place in the all-time best-sellers list, behind the Bible, the Koran and Mao Zedong's Little Red Book.

In the late 1980s, groups were given the option of allowing girls in scouting at all sections. Currently, between 5 and 10 per cent of the Scout troops in this country are mixed.

It is believed that in the last 90 years of scouting, somewhere in the region of half a billion people have been members worldwide.

TASKS

1. Try to think of one reason why boys might have joined the Scouts in 1907.
2. Can you give a reason why adults approved of the Scouts?
3. Why do you think the Scouting movement was originally for boys?
4. Why do you think there has been a gradual move to mixed-sex scouting?

The Scouts today

There are different types of scout patrol that you can join depending on how old you are:

Beavers	**6–8 years**
Cubs	**8–11 years**
Scouts/Sea Scouts/Air Scouts	**11–16 years**
Venture Scouts	**16–20 years**

If you are a Scout, you become part of a movement, a community group, a gang.

When you join a patrol, you need to prove to yourself, the patrol and the scout troop (made up of a number of local patrols) that you want to become a Scout. The first thing that you work towards is the Scout Badge. On gaining this award, you will become a Scout. There are three parts to this:

- the history of the Scout movement – how it all began
- outdoor activity – to show that you enjoy a sense of adventure and fun. This may take the form of a hike, sport or game.
- Scout Promise and Law – learning the promise and law by heart and understanding what they mean.

What do Scouts do?

The Scouts' motto is 'Be Prepared'.

This reflects the philosophy that a Scout will be able to deal with anything that could happen. Scouts work towards achieving this by training for badges. There are also some basic qualities that a person needs to become a Scout. These include:

- being practical
- being adventurous
- being good citizens
- being fun loving.

Scouts usually meet once a week. They train towards badges, they play games, they organise events. Every year, Scouts go on a camp. Camps can be held anywhere in the country and last for one week.

The Scout Law

A Scout is to be trusted.

A Scout is loyal.

A Scout is friendly and considerate.

A Scout belongs to the worldwide family of Scouts.

A Scout has courage in all difficulties.

A Scout makes good use of time and is careful of possessions and property.

A Scout has self-respect and respect for others.

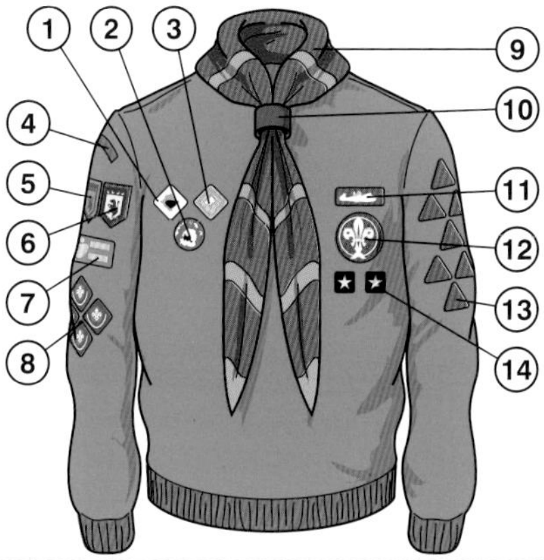

1 Adventure award	8 Scout family badges
2 Cub scout award	9 Group neckerchief
3 Adventure crest award	10 Six woggle
4 Group name tape	11 Cub scout challenge
5 District badge	12 Membership badge *(Worn over gold arrowhead)*
6 Area/county badge	13 Activity badges
7 Rank badge	14 Year stars

TASKS

1 Look at all the information on these two pages and write a list of all the good points about the Scouts – that is, what you would enjoy doing as a Scout.

2 Now write down any bad points about the Scouts – what you would not enjoy if you were a member.

Case study:
Emma Jones, 7th Willesden Scout Group

Only now when I look back on my time in the Scouts, do I realise how much of an impact it had on me. I think it taught me to be more independent and also gave me the opportunity to experience lots of different things.

I was a member of the 7th Willesden Scout Group, which was dominated mainly by boys. It was one of the first scout groups to permit the attendance of girls. I think that girls should be given this opportunity as it enables them to experience the same things as the boys do and is a way of proving that we are as able as they are. Being surrounded by boys wasn't an issue as, with regards to scouting, it was all I had known.

Being a member of the Scouts I have had the opportunity to complete the St John's Ambulance First Aid Youth Award, and to participate in 5-a-side football tournaments and swimming galas. While I was there, I completed many badges such as Athlete, Entertainer, Firefighter, and First Aid. I was awarded a 'sixer', which means someone who is leader to a small group of Scouts. I also won two trophies at camp.

When we went to camp we spent a week or two, as a troop and with others, completing badges and learning to survive outdoors. We learnt how to make a bivouac, which is a shelter made from natural materials like twigs, grass and leaves. It is built to keep you safe, warm and dry.

Being in the Scouts was something that I thoroughly enjoyed and I think gave me some advantages later in life. It taught me to be an individual and enabled me to have fun, make lots of new friends and try new things.

(With thanks to Cath and Emma Jones)

▲ Emma Jones

TASKS

1 What was different about this Scout group?

2 Describe some of the activities Emma was able to do because she was a Scout.

3 What has being a Scout meant for Emma?

Badges

Scouts train for badges to demonstrate their skills in a variety of areas. Badges that a Scout can work towards range from basketball to car maintenance, from circus skills to hip-hop, from First Aid to semaphore.

The purpose of each badge is to encourage the Scouts to learn and discover new skills and to show enthusiasm for new talents as well as enabling them to be recognised for interests and hobbies.

Sports Enthusiast Badge

1 Know the rules and laws for a sport, explain them to an examiner and be able to answer questions on specific situations.

2 Know the training levels of the sport you study and, if the sport you have chosen has a training scheme, know what is required at each stage.

3 Have a good background knowledge of the teams and sports personalities of your chosen sport.

4 State equipment required for the sport.

5 Be able to list major events for the sport of your choice.

6 Give a description of events that you have attended.

Would you be awarded the Sports Enthusiast Badge? Ask a friend to test you.

TASKS

Think about some topics that interest you. These may be to do with sport, computers, books, TV, friendship, and so on. You are going to write your own badge.

1 In pairs, agree on the badge scheme title and do the following:

a) Write out the criteria required to gain the badge – everything you need to do. These should look like a list of between 5 and 10 instructions. The instructions need to be simple and achievable.

b) Design the badge logo.

2 Now, swap around your badges and see if another pair can achieve your badge. In your pair, you should try to train towards another badge too.

You may like to record your findings in some way – either in writing or by camera.

You could also design a certificate and have a small ceremony to celebrate the class achieving various badges.

The Scout Association is always interested in hearing new ideas. You may like to get in touch with them and propose a selection of new badges.

TASK

Commercial break – advertising storyboard

A storyboard is used in advertising and marketing. Its purpose is to put across ideas and a 'vision' for an advertisement. Imagine you are a marketing designer for the Scouting Association. They have asked you to create a storyboard to show a plan for a $1\frac{1}{2}$-minute advertising campaign. The purpose of this campaign is to encourage more people to join the Scouts.

To cover the length of the advertisement, you should complete a minimum of 12 frames.

Remember that you are trying to get a visual message across but you can also use sound effects as well as words and pictures.

Try to select the most appealing and interesting elements to attract people to the Scouts. Test out your ideas on each other. Perhaps you could make the best ones into real advertisements for others to comment on.

Focus on bullying in schools

According to the charity Kidscape, between 10 and 20 per cent of the child population has experienced bullying at school. That means approximately 1.5 million schoolchildren are, or have been, affected by bullying. Some 68 per cent of children have said that being bullied is their most serious worry. This fear was rated above encounters with strangers, getting lost and child abuse.

SKILLS FOCUS

- Selecting information to support an opinion
- Finding solutions to problems

What do we mean by 'bullying'?

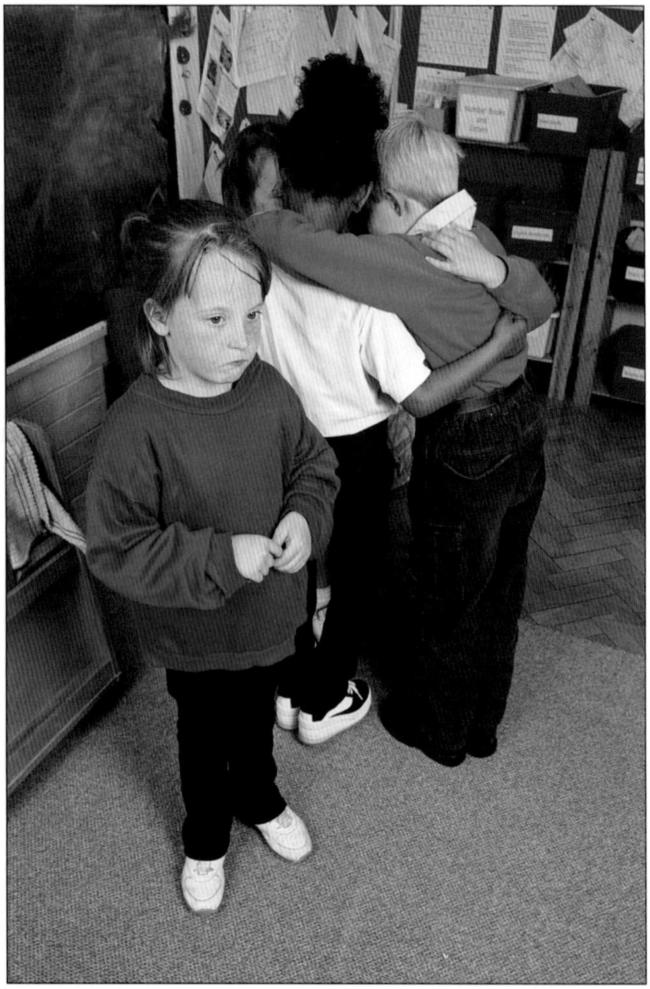

▲ **Is this girl being bullied?**

TASKS

1 List the types of action you would describe as bullying.

2 Compare your list with those of others in your class. Are there differences in the kinds of actions you described as bullying?

3 Try to agree on a definition of what bullying is. Think about what happens, why it happens and how it affects the bully and the person being bullied.

The *Collins English Dictionary* defines a bully as: 'a person who hurts, **persecutes**, or **intimidates** weaker people'.

The Department for Education and Skills (DfES) define bullying as: 'dominance of one pupil over another, or a group of others, which is planned and usually forms a pattern of behaviour rather than an isolated incident'. Bullying can include a whole range of behaviours. Among them, the DfES have identified name-calling and teasing, gossip, stealing from the victim, physical violence, threats, **coercion** and leaving pupils out of group activities.

TASK

Compare your previous definition of bullying with the information from the DfES. Discuss the ideas as a whole class and listen to as many opinions as you can. Try to come up with a statement the whole class agrees on to answer the question 'What is bullying?'

USEFUL WORDS

Persecute – To treat someone badly, especially when the action is frequently repeated

Intimidate – To scare or frighten someone

Coercion – To pressure someone into doing what you want against their wishes

Provoke – To behave in a way which causes someone else to become angry

Surveys and statistics

Kidscape Bully Survey, 1984–1986

The first national survey of bullying conducted in the UK was by the charity, Kidscape. In the survey, 4,000 children aged between 5 and 16 were interviewed.

Findings:

- 68% had been bullied at least once
- 30% had been bullied more than once
- 5% had been bullied severely
- 80% of the bullies were boys
- The majority of bullies were one year older than their victims

University of Sheffield, 1993

A survey of bullying was conducted in 21 schools in the Sheffield area over a period of $2^{1}/_{2}$ years.

Findings:

- 1 in 5 pupils reported being bullied 'now and then'
- 1 in 10 pupils reported being bullied at least 'once a week'
- Boys were almost always bullied by boys
- Girls were bullied by a mixture of boys and girls
- Most bullies were in the same class/year as their victims
- The majority of bullying took the form of teasing
- A quarter of bullying involved physical violence
- Less than half the pupils had talked to anyone about these incidents
- 1 in 8 pupils reported bullying other young people at least 'now and then'
- 1 in 25 pupils reported bullying other young people 'once a week'

Kidscape Young Offenders Survey, 1994

The survey interviewed 79 young offenders aged between 16 and 21.

Findings:

- 98% felt unchallenged bullying made pupils less respectful of authority
- 95% felt that getting away with bullying for a long time made them more likely to commit crime
- 62% of young offenders had been bullies at school
- 23% of young offenders were witnesses who had encouraged bullies
- 15% of young offenders had been victims of bullying
- Almost half of the victims had become bullies themselves
- 92% of young offenders were bullies who turned to crime
- 5% of young offenders committed crimes for bullies
- 3% of young offenders remained victims of bullies

TASKS

1 You are going to write an article about bullying. Complete the following table to help you organise the information.

Evidence that bullying is a big problem	Evidence that bullying is not a big problem

2 Choose some of the findings and try to rewrite them so they could be used for the other side of the argument.

For example, '1 in 10 pupils reported being bullied at least once a week'.

This could be rewritten as: 'Ninety per cent of young people were not bullied in their average school week'.

3 Write an article for one of these headlines. Use the information from tasks 1 and 2 to help you.

Bullying threat to young people

or

Bullying is blown up out of proportion

The bully at large

Bullying happens for many reasons. It is the victim who is left feeling frightened and worthless. But the bully is also likely to be reacting to a situation that has affected them emotionally.

Why bully?

A scapegoat at home

Low self-esteem

Enjoys power

Suffered abuse

Unable to empathise (see things from others point of view)

Insecure

Not academically bright or able

Change in family circumstance, eg divorce

Spoilt: used to getting his or her own way

Who is the bully?

Research has shown that there are different types of bully.

Anxious bullies
- Lack confidence
- Experienced 'failure' at home or in school
- Coward or 'hanger on'

Boys and girls
- Boy bullies tend to be more destructive and violent than girls
- Girl bullies tend to use gossip, name-calling and ignore people

Age
- Primary-school pupils are twice as likely to bully as secondary-school students
- There is less bullying after 13 years of age

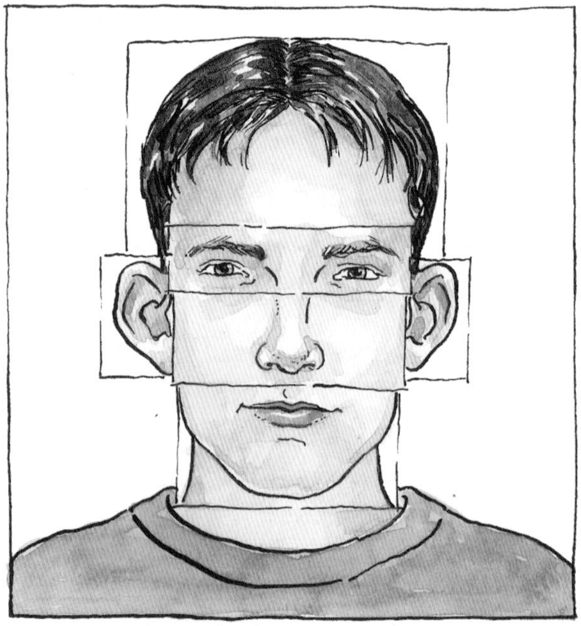

Bullies
- Physically stronger
- More energy and confidence
- Enjoy conflict and aggression
- Seek situations where people can see their aggression
- BUT they often lose popularity in their teens

Why did you become a bully?
- 'It made me feel big in front of my friends'
- 'I did it to show off'
- 'I wanted to show the girls who was best'
- 'I was a nobody at home but at school I was Top-Dog and that was great!'

The victim

There are many types of people who experience being bullied. Just as every bully is not the same, every victim is different too. It is important to recognise that some people provoke bullies, but that most victims do not.

Who is the victim?

Passive victim
- Avoids aggression and conflict
- Lacks confidence
- Physically weaker
- Shy and nervous

Provocative victim
- Teases and taunts others
- Quick to complain if others speak back
- 15 per cent of victims fall into this category

Victims who play along
- Plays up to being a victim to gain friends
- Class clown
- Hides their ability
- Attention seeking

Bully victim
- Some victims become bullies themselves
- Some who have strict home lives bully at school for a 'release'

What happens to the victims?

Bullying affects children differently. For some young people it can become unbearable and 10 children commit suicide every year because of bullying. Many others play truant or pretend to be ill to avoid the bully at school.

There are many reasons why bullying stops. Sometimes it just stops as children get older, or it may stop because of the actions of the victim. Many victims get help and support from friends, family, teachers and others and this often ends the period of bullying.

TASKS

1 a) Draw a picture of a bully and their victim.

b) Describe the characters you have drawn.

c) Add a thought bubble showing what each character is thinking.

2 For each character, describe an action they could take to end the situation.

3 Describe an action their friends could take to improve the situation.

4 What could the school do to improve the situation?

If you are the victim of bullying and need to talk to someone, you can phone Childline on 0800 1111. All calls are confidential and free.

TAKING IT FURTHER

In pairs or groups, develop a role play about bullies, bullying and how to overcome it. This could form part of an anti-bullying campaign.

‘The camera never lies’

▲ Tuesday 4 September:
10:22 morning break

▼ Tuesday 4 September:
10:28 morning break

TASKS

1 Study the photographs carefully. They were printed from a CCTV camera at a school which has a bullying problem. Describe what you see in each of the photos. Use the following points to help you:

- what do you think has happened?
- do you think it is an example of bullying?
- who is the bully and who is the victim?

You may like to work in groups initially to make some kind of judgement. Discuss your ideas with others, before forming a conclusion.

2 Write up ‘Witness Statements’ for the following people:

- the bullies
- the victim
- the teacher

▲ **Tuesday 4 September: 10:33 morning break**

▼ **Tuesday 4 September: 10:36 end of break**

Think about the different thoughts of each of these people. Include information about what happened, what had happened before the incident and anything that has occurred since. Try to use as much detail as possible.

3 In groups, draw up an anti-bullying policy for this school. Think about your earlier definition of bullying and all the information you have about different types of bullying. Discuss your ideas with other groups in the class and agree on one overall policy for the school. You may like to submit it to your Head of Year.

4 Write down what might have happened next in the sequence of photographs if the school had adopted your anti-bullying policy.

Using the media

What is the media?

We all have an idea about what is meant by the word '**media**'. Pop stars and other famous people are forever complaining about the media ignoring their **right to privacy**. The term 'media' includes television and radio, at a local, national and international level. It also includes magazines and newspapers of all sorts with circulations ranging from under 100 to well over a million. More recently, the development of electronic technology has been responsible for the creation of a whole new medium – the Internet.

SKILLS FOCUS

- Planning a campaign
- Understanding different writing styles

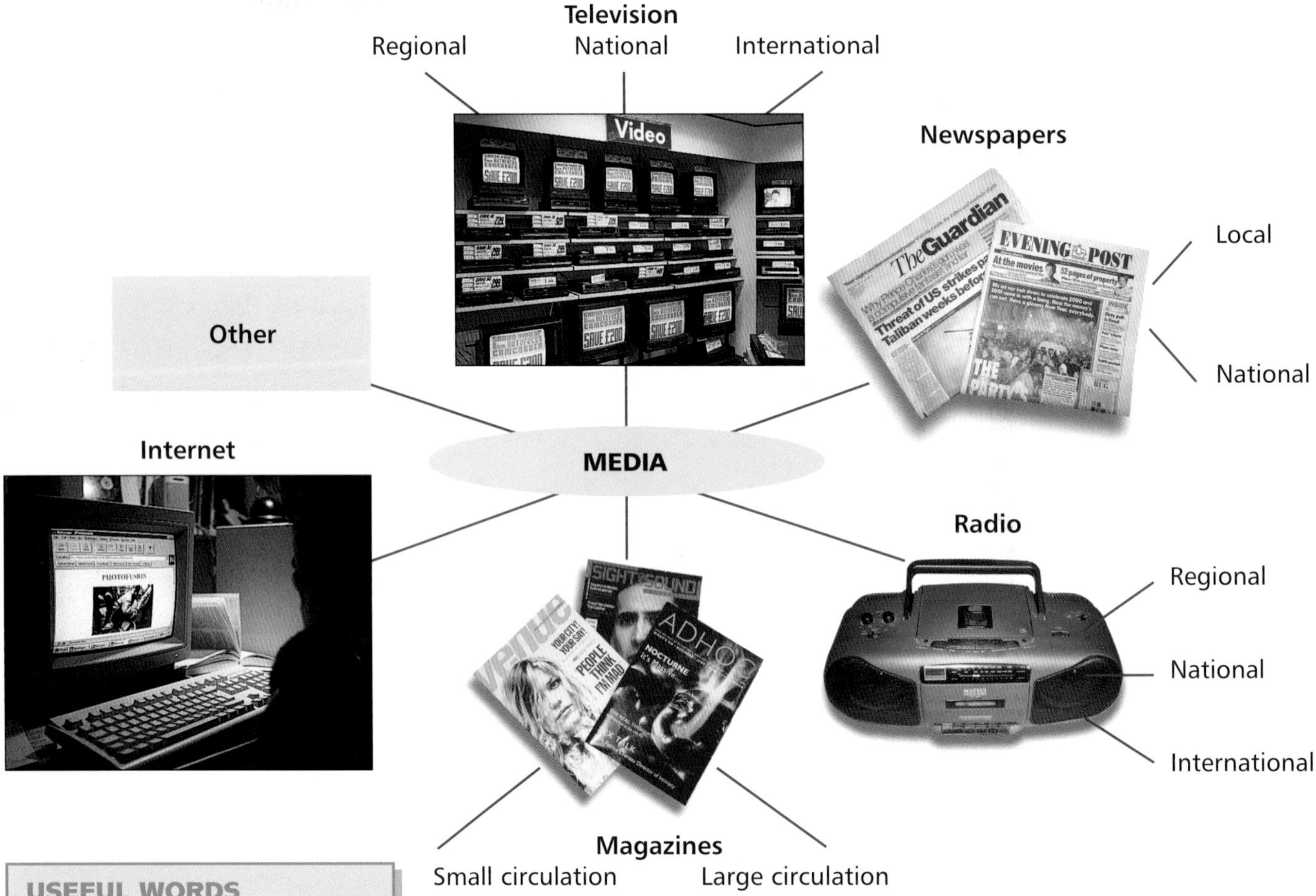

USEFUL WORDS

Media – A way of communicating with people

Right to privacy – We all have a right to a private life. There is much debate about whether the media violates that right if they publish stories about us

Campaign – A series of activities to help achieve an end goal or cause a change

TASKS

1. Copy the diagram about media onto a sheet of paper and add in examples for each category.
2. In what ways is the Internet similar to the other media? In what ways is it different?
3. What do you use media for? Brainstorm all the uses you can think of, then combine them in a class list.
4. Do all people use media for the same reasons?

Different media are particularly good for different purposes. Look at the following examples of information and decide which of the media might suit which example.

A new type of crane has been designed that will speed up the construction of medium-sized buildings. Experts claimed that construction time could be cut by up to 10%.

▲ **Story 1: Specialist information (information that is likely to appeal only to people interested in that particular subject; such people may live far away from each other).**

BREAKING NEWS!

An earthquake has devastated San Salvador, a city in Central America. Many people have been injured or killed and many buildings destroyed. No English-speaking people are available for interview at the moment.

▲ **Story 2: Current affairs (information that has a wide appeal but only for a short period of time).**

The police have responded to the government's new Crime Reduction package. It involves increased spending, new training programmes and closer communication with victim-support groups. The police spokesman broadly supported the ideas but had specific concerns.

▲ **Story 3: Complicated financial or political details (information that has quite a wide appeal but takes careful and long explanation).**

There is a busy day of national athletics trials taking place. The names of competitors, clubs and details of past performances are included in the biggest survey of its kind.

▲ **Story 4: Sports information (information that needs to be delivered quickly but can be lengthy, detailed and complicated too; can appeal to a reasonably large number of people but certainly not everybody).**

TASK

1 Using the four stories above complete the following table. For each story decide which medium would be the best to use to communicate the information and put a 1 in the column. Label the next best medium 2, and so on down to 5.

	Story 1	Story 2	Story 3	Story 4
Internet				
Radio				
Newspaper				
Television				
Magazines				

2 Do you think that one medium is better than the others?

Looking at newspapers

So far you have been looking at the media in a very general way, comparing the strengths and weaknesses of the different types in different situations. This page looks specifically at newspapers.

Newspapers are by far the oldest of the different media you have looked at. The first national daily newspaper, *The Times*, was published as long ago as 1788. People read a newspaper for many reasons, and many people rely on newspapers of one sort or another to provide all kinds of information.

Unscramble the words on the opposite drawing. Each one describes a feature of a newspaper someone might use.

Which of these sections would you use in a newspaper? Which areas would you not read at all? Why?

Not all newspapers are the same, in fact they often look very different. They can be different sizes and aim at a different readership too. The next activity is designed to help you think in more detail about different types of newspaper.

DIFFERENT TYPES OF NEWSPAPER

Read the following extracts and match them up with the sort of newspaper you think they may have come from:

EXTRACT	NEWSPAPER TYPE
A: There has been a recent increase in the number of 15-25 year olds attending Church services. The Reverend John Robertson called the increase 'small but significant'.	Specialist sports
B: Jill Bankley, of Romford, has won a place in the quarter-finals of the National Amateur Ladies Golf Championships. Mrs Bankley, a teacher at a local school, is said to be 'delighted'.	Advertisements paper
C: A tornado, with winds reaching more than 100 miles per hour, has swept through the midwestern states of America.	Church paper
D: In one of today's smaller race meetings, the young horse, Flyn's Flyer, is expected to upset the favourite (Ripon 2:00pm).	National daily paper
E: Room to let. Would suit working individual who doesn't smoke. £80 per week.	Local paper

Comparing national and local newspapers

Different types of newspaper select the information they communicate depending upon their readership: that is, who their readers are and what they are interested in. The most important factor they have to consider is whether their readership is local or national.

Below you will see two extracts relating to one story. Read them carefully before deciding which article came from a local newspaper and which one came from a national newspaper. Write a couple of lines explaining the reasons behind your decisions.

Article 1
Weather Chaos Costs Farmers £500m

Parts of Britain are back on flood alert after fresh downpours across the country yesterday, while farmers estimated the bad weather had already cost them millions of pounds this winter. The number of flood warnings in England and Wales rose by three overnight to 32, the agency added. Nationally, the situation was stable.

The severe weather has cost farmers an estimated £500m in uninsured losses of crops and property, according to the National Farmers' Union. The NFU said around 13% of the national potato crop – some 822,200 tonnes – had been destroyed or remained in the ground almost two months after the first deluge, at a possible cost of £97m. The cereal and sugar beet crops had suffered similar fates.

The NFU said the total loss to the industry, including damage to buildings, was likely to top £500m. Union president Ben Gill said, 'These figures confirm our worst fears. Some farmers have had almost their entire business wiped out.'

Article 2
The Day The Rains Came

Residents were plunged into misery this week as the River Roding burst its banks following Sunday's storm. Over 300 properties have been affected by the floods and 40 people were evacuated from their homes on Monday.

The storm, now being hailed as the Great Storm of 2000, caused the Roding to burst its banks in three places on Monday morning, flooding an area of three square miles.

Problem areas along the river are Chingford Road, Roding Lane South and Wanstead Park Road, where the flooding is at its worst.

Gordon and Gillian Baxter were evacuated from their home at 3am Tuesday. Gillian said: 'It was up to my knees and flowing uphill. The police told us that we had to leave because another three feet and the pumping station opposite would have blown up and smashed all the windows.'

A council spokesman said: 'We have opened up an emergency rest centre at Caterham High school where 12 spent the night.'

TASK

Writing for a national or a local readership

Either:

Find a national story and rewrite it for a local paper (you may have to make up some additional facts).

Or

Find a local story and rewrite it to make it interesting for a national newspaper (you will have to think carefully about which story you choose here).

Show the examples you have written to someone else in the class. Do you both agree that you have changed the focus of the article enough? You could even write out both stories and ask people to guess which is the local newspaper article and which is the national newspaper article to see how well you have done.

TAKING IT FURTHER

You could do a project comparing the national and local press or TV news. What similarities are there, and what differences?

Article 1: adapted from Keith Perry, *The Guardian*, Saturday 6 January, 2001
Article 2: adapted from front page story, *Ilford & Redbridge Free Post*, week ending 4/11/00, by Chris Panteli

Using the media

Road-safety campaign

The situation

Kevin McCall was knocked down in a road accident. The accident could have been prevented if there had been a crossing and road signs before the bend. Kevin was taken into hospital and his parents, friends and neighbours met to form an action committee to **campaign** for road improvements. They wanted to make sure similar accidents would be avoided in future.

First attempts

The group met to discuss what they wanted. They all agreed that they had to get road signs and a crossing. Billy, who knows some people in the council, agreed to follow up his contacts. His friend in the Roads Service was unable to help and even his other friend, Councillor Jones, was not encouraging. They both thought that it would be too expensive to make the changes the group wanted, and the council did not have enough money.

The next steps

After their first attempt to persuade the council to make the road improvements had failed, the group decided they needed to involve more people in their campaign. They started to do this with a petition and by getting in touch with other local groups. They also decided they were going to try to use the media for their own purposes. They organised a demonstration at the town hall when the next council meeting was due to take place. Then they invited the local press along and told them they were going to challenge the councillors over their decision. Obviously the press thought this could be interesting and they turned up to see what happened ...

▲ The new recruits to the campaign turned up

▲ The organisers were able to put their message across to the journalists

▲ The councillors were challenged in public over their decision

TASK

Imagine you are a journalist following the story. You want to make people aware of what happened to Kevin and tell them about his friends' actions. You turned up at the town hall and saw the demonstration and interviewed some of the people there. Now you must produce a story for the front page of your local newspaper or a report for the local radio station.

Help Box

For each type of media think about how you can grab attention, how to structure the story, and how to explain the different points of view. There will be different techniques for newspapers and radio.

What did happen?

The plan worked. The media picked up the story and the councillors were put under pressure. Even the local MP supported the group. In this case the media really helped the local group achieve what they wanted.

What if it had not worked?

Of course, it is not always so easy to use the media like this. If something else had happened at the last minute, such as a bank robbery at the other end of town, the journalists might have gone to report that story instead. If the councillors had left by the back door the story might not have been exciting enough to get into the news. But that does not mean that the group would have had to give up their struggle. There are many other measures they could have taken to raise awareness.

Here are some of the other ideas the group discussed, with the problems they thought of for each.

More action (meeting notes)

(1) Paint our own crossing on the road and put up our own home-made signs
What are the arguments for and against this idea?

(2) Letter-writing
Who should we write to? Who could help?

(3) Posters
What could they say? Where should we put them?

(4) Another petition
What should we do with it once it is complete?

(5) Stunts to get media coverage
What could we do?

TASKS

1. Copy out the list and try to answer the questions for each point.
2. Add any other ideas you can think of for action the group could have taken.

TAKING IT FURTHER

Are there any local issues you would like to take action about?

Look at your local newspapers.

a) Are there any local issues or campaigns being written about?

b) How interesting is your local paper?

c) Do you have any good news you would like your local newspaper to cover? Discuss this as a class. If you can agree on a good idea phone the paper or write them a letter inviting them to find out more.

The world on your doorstep

Your local area, be it a village, a town or part of a city, is connected to the wider world in very many different ways. Sometimes your local community might not be obviously associated with other countries, but there is always a chain of connections linking you with the wider world. A shoe made in India, for example, might not have come straight off a plane into a shop on your high street. The shoe is much more likely to be delivered to a warehouse first, before ending up on the shelf in a shop down the road from you.

SKILLS FOCUS

- Think about your actions
- Developing an opinion

▼ Some of Jane's links to the world

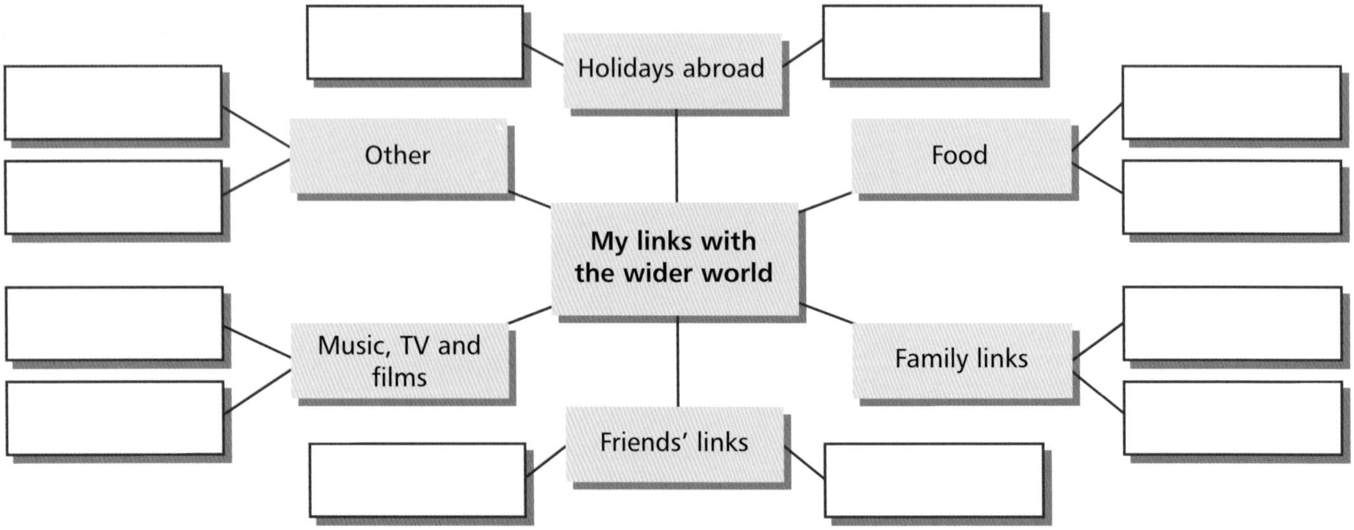

TASK

Look at the picture opposite. It gives you some clues about the ways in which you may be connected to the wider world. Once you have studied the picture, copy and complete the spider diagram above. Add as many examples as you can for yourself. Then you could add in the connections for your friends and family in another colour. Finally, you could produce a whole-class version showing all your links with the wider world.

HSBC Bank
OXFAM
GO SPORTS
COMPUTERS'R'US
Baseball bats and gloves
Real Madrid football shirts
Trainers
Golf clubs
Hand stitched footballs
PS2
DVD
TAJ MAHAL curry house
All you can eat for £6 lunch special
GLOBAL ADVENTURE travel agents
USA fly drive
India
JAPAN
Tenerife golfing weekends
France daytrips
South African Safari
Thailand
Newsagent
Cheap calls from here anywhere in world
chocolate special offer
cassava
mangos
Cape grapes
French apples
Israeli oranges
GLOBAL WARMING FEAR GROWS
Coke
Mars
McDonald's

Global shopping

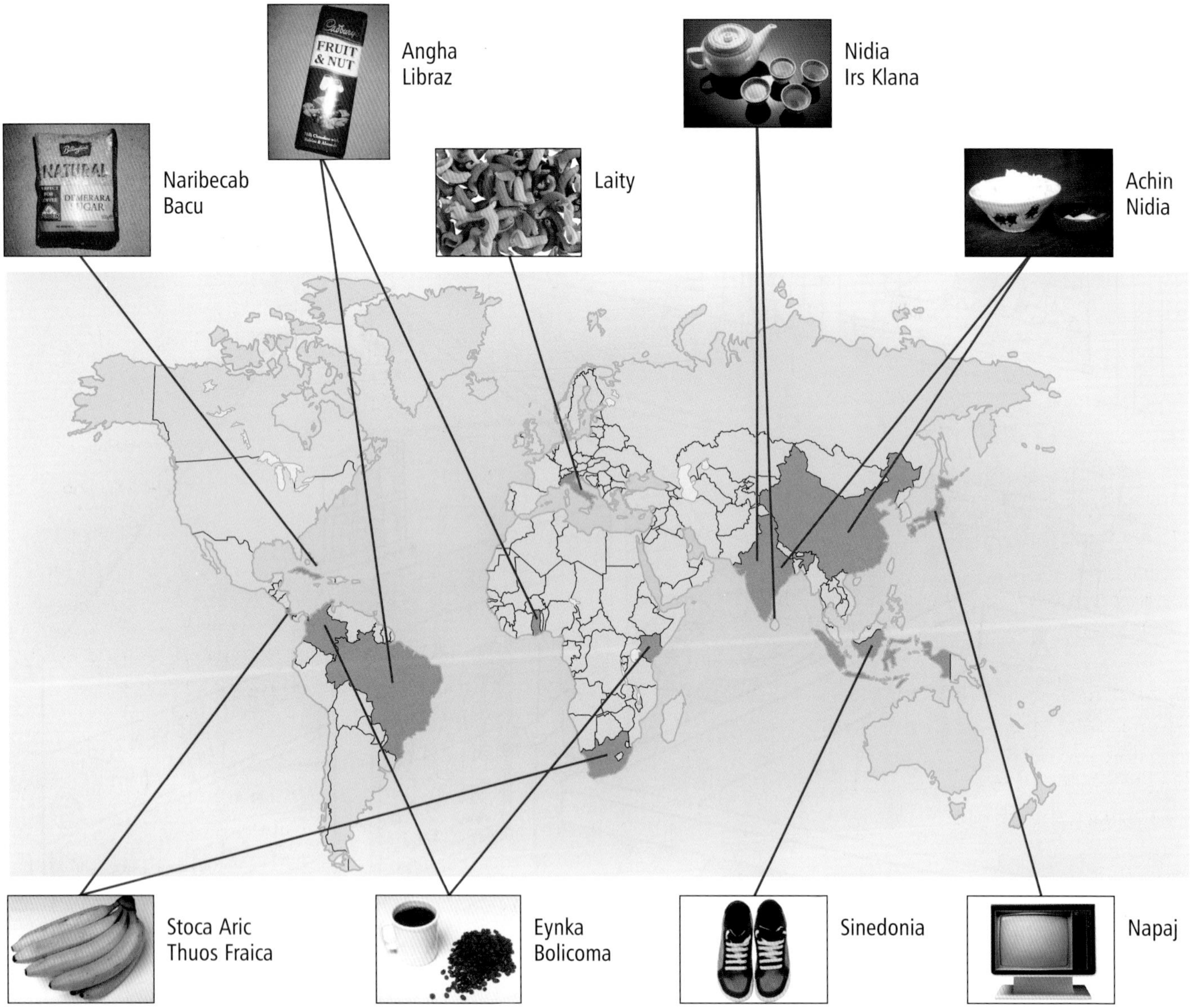

TASKS

1 Unscramble the words to find out where the products come from (you may need to use an atlas to help you).

2 Copy and complete the table below. As well as the products listed above, can you think of any others?

3 Describe what your table shows.

4 Has it always been possible to have such easy access to a wide variety of products?

Product	Name of country	Other products from that country
Tea	*India*	*Cotton*
		Rice
		Spices

Divine inspiration

▲ **We often think about chocolate, but have you ever wondered where it comes from and how it is made?**

Being connected to the world means we can have luxuries such as chocolate whenever we want. But the decisions we make about how we spend our money have a knock-on effect all around the world. Think about that chocolate bar for a moment.

▲ **Cocoa beans are grown in developing countries, such as Ghana**

Fair-trade chocolate – where does your £1.35 go?

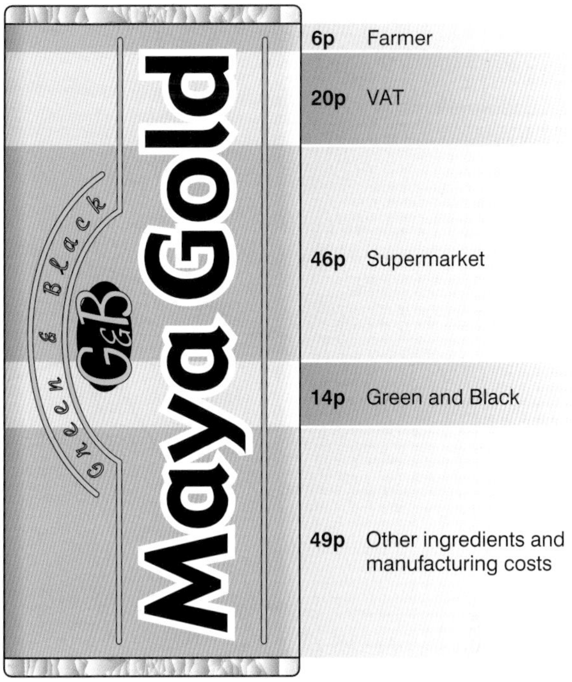

If you spent £1.35 on an ordinary bar of milk chocolate the farmer would get less than 1 pence for it.

TASKS

1. What brand of chocolate do you normally buy?
2. Why do you choose that brand?
3. Have you ever thought about the people who helped to produce the chocolate?
4. Do you think they receive enough money for producing the cocoa?
5. If you had the choice would you rather have fair-trade chocolate or regular chocolate?

TAKING IT FURTHER

Ask other people how much they think the cocoa farmer would receive from the sale of a £1.35 bar of chocolate.

Go to your local sweet shop and supermarket to see how many brands of chocolate there are in total and how many are fair trade.

Why do you think some chocolate is not fairly traded?

Sustainable links?

ADVANTAGES

Holidays
(Give an opportunity to see how other people live around the world)

Work abroad
(You can share your skills with other people who may not have access to the same training or education)

Charity

Shopping

Music

Air travel
(It is getting cheaper to travel around the world)

Clothes

TASK

Explaining the picture

- What does the picture show you?
- What message do you think the artist was trying to get across?
- Do you agree with the artist?
- Draw your own cartoon of your links to the world.

DISADVANTAGES

Holidays
(Some holiday activities destroy the local cultures and environments, eg diving can kill the coral reefs)

Work abroad

Charity
(Just giving people money alone does not tackle the real root of their problems)

Shopping
(Many workers in developing countries do not get fair wages for producing the goods we buy in our shops)

Music
(British and American music can sometimes replace local traditional music)

Clothes
(Clothes are often made in factories around the world where working conditions are terrible)

TASKS

1 Write a sentence for each of the spaces around the picture of the globe.
2 Which statements do you agree with?
3 Which statements do you disagree with?
4 Think of a way to overcome each of the disadvantages.
5 Discuss your answers with others in the class.
6 What do you think of all these global links? Do they make your life better? Do they make everyone's life better? (Give reasons for your answers.)

Writing your project

Before you start a big project it is useful spending some time working out how you are going to organise it. Read through the following stages and think about your answers for each one. By the time you reach the bottom of this page you should be able to write a plan for your project and know how you are going to get it done.

✓ Choose a topic you are interested in

Stage 1: Choose a topic

It is important to have a clear focus for your project. You may have to decide with your teacher what focus your project will have. Otherwise you could look through the rest of this book and find ideas. It could be a broad topic, such as 'children's rights', or a very specific topic, like 'bullying'.

✓ Take your time to find a clear focus

Stage 2: Find a focus

You need to be clear exactly what your project is about. This may involve narrowing the focus of the project. This is more important when your topic is very broad, but it is also useful for specific topics too. Think of a title that says exactly what you are looking at or a question you would like to answer. Here are a couple of examples:

Topic: Children's rights
Focus: United Nations Convention on the Rights of the Child
Question: How much do students in my school know about their rights?

Topic: Bullying
Focus: Bullying in my school
Question: What does the school do about bullying and does it work?

✓ Do not rely on one source of information

Remember the difference between facts and opinions

Stage 3: Finding information

There are plenty of ideas at the beginning of this book about where to find information. Try to use a variety of sources. For example, you could try the following:

- Surveys – you could pass around questionnaires to people or interview them face to face to find out their experiences or opinions.
- Internet – use the links on the next few pages or search engines to find useful information. Using a search engine will be easier if you are already clear what your project is about.
- Printed sources – Other books, magazines and newspapers may cover your topic. Even if the project is about your school you may be able to find some useful background information in other places.

✓ Break up your text with titles, graphs and pictures

Stage 4 – Organising the information

It is important to make the most of the information you have collected. Do not just copy all the useful information you find out or write out the results of your interviews. Think about the way you present the information. Consider how the information helps you answer the question you set at the beginning of the project, or how it fits with your title.

✓ Read the whole of the project first to make sure the conclusion fits with the rest of your work

Stage 5: Conclusion

At the end of the project try to sum up what you have discovered. You can either write down what you think about the issue in the title or sum up your answer to the question. This is the place where you have to say what you think about the topic. Remember to give reasons for your opinions.

Suggestions for projects

Chapter 2: Rights and responsibilities
Organisations for young people's rights

Suggested titles:

How much do young people know about their rights?

Does your school meet young people's rights?

Do young people feel their rights are respected?

Young people's rights around the world – do we all have the same rights?

Useful web-links:

www.unicef.org/crc
United Nations Convention on the Rights of the Child

www.carelaw.org.uk
Rights of young people in care

www.article12.org
Rights organisation for young people

www.carnegie-youth.org.uk
Information about how the Carnegie Trust works to get young people's views recognised

www.cre.gov.uk
The Commission for Racial Equality's website with information about your rights

www.un.org/pubs/cyberschoolbus
United Nations website aimed at young people with plenty of information about rights around the world

www.scfuk.org.uk
Save the Children UK

Chapter 3: Diversity
Sources of information and campaign groups

Suggested titles:

Does your school achieve equal opportunities?

How can we tackle racism or sexism?

What can be done to promote equal opportunities?

Does everyone understand what equal opportunities means for them?

Useful web-links:

www.cre.gov.uk
Commission for Racial Equality

www.eoc.org.uk
Equal Opportunities Commission looking at gender equality

www.ayme.org.uk
Information about a campaign group for children suffering from M.E.

www.sortit.org.uk
Aimed at young people with impaired sight

www.byc.org.uk
British Youth Council website for young people's action

www.homebeats.co.uk
Institute of Race Relations for news, quizzes and links

Chapter 4: Government services
Local government

Suggested titles:

What does local government do?

Do people know about local government?

How good a job does your local government do?

Useful web-links:

www.lgiu.gov.uk
The Local Government Information Unit has some news and also links to many related sites

www.open.gov.uk
This website has links to many local government sites as well as information about what local government does

www.dfee.gov.uk
This site has a search engine for your postcode so that you can check out how schools in your area are performing

www.psr.keele.ac.uk/local.htm
Background information and a link to every local government website

www.lga.gov.uk
Plenty of background information about local government to download

Chapter 5: Democracy
Local democracy

Suggested topics:

What do councillors do?

How many adults voted for councillors in your area and why?

Who runs the local council?

How do people know what is happening in the council?

How good is our democracy?

Useful web-links:

www.local-government.net
A useful general website

www.gwynedd.gov.uk
www.sheffield.gov.uk
www.hants.gov.uk
Some examples of how councils are using websites

www.explore.parliament.uk
A student-friendly site looking at parliament, with information and quizzes

www.charter88.org.uk
This site looks at how our system of voting works and campaigns for changes

Chapter 6: Community groups

Suggested topics:

What community groups are there in your area?

How do LETS work?

Could you set up your own LETS scheme?

What community groups do people you know belong to?

Why do people join community groups?

Useful web-links:

www.southcote.net
An example of a website run for community groups

www.pcthorpe.freeserve.co.uk
www.g-vis.co.uk/gvls
Local Exchange Trade Schemes

www.scoutbase.org.uk
www.guides.org.uk
Two examples of young people's community groups

Chapter 7: Resolving conflict

Bullying

Suggested topics:

How common is bullying in your school?

Does bullying change between primary and secondary schools?

Is there a difference between boys and girls in terms of bullying?

How does your school compare to other places?

Do we do enough about bullying?

Useful web-links:

www.bullying.co.uk
www.antibullying.net
www.successunlimited.co.uk
Three useful websites exploring issues related to bullying in and outside school. Each website has plenty of helpful links

www.childline.org.uk
There is a useful section aimed at young people with a series of fact sheets about bullying

www.nspcc.org.uk
The National Society for the Prevention of Cruelty to Children. Use the search engine to look for information on bullying

Chapter 8: Media

Suggested topics:

How does your local newspaper compare to national newspapers?

How are local and national TV similar or different?

Do people use local or national media more often?

What are the advantages and disadvantages of local media?

Useful web-links:

www.the-times.co.uk
www.guardian.co.uk
www.telegraph.co.uk
www.independent.co.uk
www.news.bbc.co.uk
Some examples of national media organisations

www.thisisgloucestershire.co.uk
www.dyw.ndirect.co.uk
Local newspaper links and examples

Chapter 9: Global community

Suggested topics:

How effective is fair trade?

How are we linked to the world?

How do our actions affect other people around the world?

How does your local area reflect the diversity around the world?

What do people know about their global links?

Useful web-links

www.oxfam.org.uk/fair_trade.html
www.fairtrade.org.uk
www.greendirect.co.uk
www.ontheline.org.uk/schools/chocbix/home.htm
www.afrikatrading.co.uk
Examples of websites promoting fair trade

www.panda.org
The World Wildlife Trust website looks at the links between us and our environment around the world

www.oxfam.org.uk
Click on Cool Planet for a useful website aimed at young people and full of information about global connections

Glossary

Budget – The amount of money available to spend over a given period of time

Campaign – A series of activities to help achieve an end goal or cause a change

Coercion – To pressure someone into doing what you want against their wishes

Community group – Any group which brings people together voluntarily

Convention – An agreement between several countries

Court injunction – An instruction from the court to stop doing something

Democracy – Government by the people

Direct democracy – People make decisions directly themselves

Discrimination – Behaving differently towards people because they are different to you in some way

Diversity – The differences between us

Education Action Zone (EAZ) – Areas where achievement is low can get extra money for their schools if they become an EAZ

Equal opportunities – Everyone has the same chance of achieving success

Inclusive – Accepting everyone's differences and trying to provide equal opportunities

Intimidate – To scare or frighten someone

Local Education Authority (LEA) – The LEA shares out the money from government to schools and helps schools

Local Exchange Trade Schemes (LETS) – Local groups of people who exchange goods and services with each other for no money

Media – A way of communicating with people

Persecute – To treat someone badly, especially when the action is frequently repeated

Provoke – To behave in a way which causes someone else to become angry

Representative democracy – People choose someone to represent them in government

Resolve – Solve a problem or sort out a difficult situation by reaching agreement

Right to privacy – We all have a right to a private life. There is much debate about whether the media violates that right if they publish stories about us

Treasury – The government department that collects taxes and decides what services the money gets spent on

Violate – Break someone else's rights

Index